Distinguished American Jews

CONTRIBUTORS TO THIS VOLUME

EDWIN T. RANDALL
Pastor, Monticello Community Church, Monticello, Minnesota

HAROLD B. HUNTING
Pastor, Congregational Church, Greenfield, New Hampshire

IVAN GEROULD GRIMSHAW
American International College, Springfield, Massachusetts

MYRTLE LECKY GRIMSHAW
Author and Reviewer

GRACE CHAPIN AUTEN
Author and Teacher, Champaign, Illinois

KARL R. STOLZ
Formerly Dean of the Hartford School of Religious Education

KENDIG BRUBAKER CULLY
*Pastor, Melrose Highlands Congregational Church,
Melrose, Massachusetts*

P. HENRY LOTZ
Pastor, Methodist Church, Toulon, Illinois

Distinguished American Jews

EDITED BY

PHILIP HENRY LOTZ

EUGENE SHEDDEN FARLEY LIBRARY

WILKES COLLEGE, WILKES-BARRE, PA.

REMOVED FROM
E. S. FARLEY LIBRARY
WILKES UNIVERSITY
COLLECTION
1983

Essay Index Reprint Series

BOOKS FOR LIBRARIES PRESS
FREEPORT, NEW YORK

Originally published as Volume VI of the
Creative Personalities Series

Copyright © 1945 by The International Committee of
Young Men's Christian Associations

Reprinted 1970 by arrangement with Association Press

E184
J5L78

STANDARD BOOK NUMBER:
8369-1671-9

LIBRARY OF CONGRESS CATALOG CARD NUMBER:
78-111842

PRINTED IN THE UNITED STATES OF AMERICA

Contents

160463

Introduction

by

PHILIP HENRY LOTZ

Let us now praise famous men,
And our fathers that begat us.
The Lord manifested in them great glory,
Even his mighty power from the beginning.
Such as did bear rule in their kingdoms,
And were men renowned for their power,
Giving counsel by their understanding,
Such as have brought tidings in prophecies:
Leaders of the people by their counsels,
And by their understanding men of learning for the people;
Wise were their words in their instruction:
Such as sought out musical tunes,
And set forth verses in writing:
Rich men furnished with ability,
Living peaceably in their habitations:
All these were honored in their generations,
And were a glory in their days.

PERHAPS NOWHERE has the far-flung influence for good of great and noble men been better summed up than in these words from the Apocrypha. They are taken from Ecclesiasticus, part of the great religious literature of the Jewish people.

"The Jewish people is one of the oldest living religious groups in the world. It dates its origin back 3500 years. Throughout the centuries, it has made unique and distinct contributions to humanity and to the world. Its contributions have been not only in the fields of religion, where it has felt itself strongest, but likewise in all fields of endeavor." This paragraph is quoted from *Syllabus on Jewish Contributions to Civilization,* The Temple High School of The Temple.

This volume of Distinguished American Jews includes a journalist, a nurse, a statesman, a rabbi, a scientist, a writer, an actor, a violinist, a doctor, a motion-picture producer, a founder of a movement, and a justice of the Supreme Court. The Jew has made his own unique contribution in medicine and science, music, literature, law, philanthropy and religion. How many men have prudently crept into nameless graves, while these personalities have forgotten themselves into eternity.

There are probably four and a half million Jews in America. They are one of the smallest religious and racial groups and yet they have probably produced more great men than any other group in the history of America.

"I am passionately anxious to awake in people in general a sensitiveness to small people."—Fannie Hurst.

"I want to thank you for your smile," said Einstein to Lillian Wald when visiting her in her home in Westport, Connecticut.

"When Rabbi Wise attacks a politician, steamship business to Europe improves immediately," said Mayor LaGuardia at a banquet in honor of the sixtieth birthday of Rabbi Wise.

These brief quotations suggest interesting characteristics of only a few of the persons to be considered. Many of these Jewish leaders remind us of the prophets of the Old Testament. They are filled with a sense of mission to downtrodden men and women They are filled with zeal to secure justice and opportunity fo. all men.

Anti-Semitism is abroad in the world, not only in Europe but also in America. The Jew is made the scapegoat. He is accused of crucifying Jesus nineteen hundred years ago; of dominating the economic life of the nation; of being responsible for this war; and so on, through the whole category of evils. Recently Jewish boys have been beaten and mistreated in some of the larger cities. American democracy and Christianity, when true to themselves, believe in and must advocate the brotherhood of all men.

It is our sincere hope that the presentation of these great Jewish characters will make a contribution to better cultural relations between Gentiles and Jews. Perhaps it will help us to understand better that we, too, are "debtors to all men," not the least to the Jews.

The editor desires to express his deep appreciation to all who have helped in the making and distribution of this volume.

Toulon, Illinois.   PHILIP HENRY LOTZ.
September, 1944.

Adolph Simon Ochs

Merchant of News

by

Edwin T. Randall

Be noble! and the nobleness that lies
In other men, sleeping, but never dead,
Will rise in majesty to meet thine own;
Then wilt thou see it gleam in many eyes,
Then will pure light around thy path be shed,
And thou wilt nevermore be sad and lone.

—James Russell Lowell

AT THE EARLY AGE OF TEN Adolph Ochs began work at what was to be his lifetime vocation, selling news. His influence upon United States journalism was significant, not only because of his own great talents and towering personality, but because he came onto the scene at the very time when the newspaper business was making the change by which it became a strictly commercial affair.

In the early days, newspapers exercised some of the functions of the pulpit. They informed the people of what was going on and also interpreted events; and often quite definitely suggested courses of action in relation to public problems. Each paper had its own definite point of view and was constantly impressing that point of view upon its readers. Its purpose was the interest of its readers and the public welfare. It was upon this basis that the strict regulations were made which guarantee the freedom of the press. But it must be remembered that this freedom was freedom from government control.

Within a generation after the Civil War, small stores began to

1

combine into great department stores. Whereas, competition between many small stores was narrowly restricted because of limited
resources, competition between enormous and growing department
stores became something else; something powerful and, at times,
sinister.

These department stores began advertising in the newspapers
in a big way. Once the advertisements had been hidden among
news items, just a line or two for each place of business, similar to
our modern want ads. But as the department stores advertised
more and more "bargains," that process began which ended in
enormous quantities of advertising—often with news items almost
hidden among the ads. This required enlargement of space, and
papers began to be printed on "pulp" paper (as they are today)
instead of on "rag" paper (as books are printed).

Circulation became the matter of greatest importance. More
and more of the expense of publishing papers was assumed by the
advertisers and profits depended wholly upon the income from the
advertising department. But advertisers cared only about how many
people read their announcements, so the objective of the newspaper
changed subtly to a desire to secure the largest possible circulation
—and, in consequence, the largest possible advertising income.
Thus the newspaper became a commercial enterprise.

You can easily understand that the fight for circulation in such
a city as New York brought about some interesting situations. In
1835, James Gordon Bennett started a paper with a total capital
of $500, two wooden chairs and an old dry-goods box. It was he
who, sometime afterward, discovered the sales value of scandal
and built up his circulation by publishing the sort of things that,
in a small town, circulate only by word of mouth. Fifteen years
later, it took more than a hundred thousand dollars to establish a
paper, the *New York Times*.

Development continued, though changes took place rather
slowly, and it was not until the last of the nineteenth century that
the struggle for circulation really became intense. Joseph Pulitzer
was one of the kings of what was called "yellow journalism."
In 1896, William Randolph Hearst came from San Francisco,
where he had made a remarkable success of one newspaper, to

enter the struggle. He discovered the sales value of war to a newspaper and sold to the United States the idea of the Spanish-Ameri-
can War.

But the very same year, there came also to the city of New York
a man of an entirely different type and of perhaps even greater
journalistic genius. He entered the struggle against some of the
newspaper financial giants of the nation, unostentatiously and
with a sure feeling for the fundamental decency of the American
people. His name was Adolph Simon Ochs.

What was his preparation for so great a task? What was his
genius?

He was born March 12, 1858, in Cincinnati, of well-educated
Jewish parents who had emigrated to America in their youth.
Julius Ochs, the father, had served as an officer in the Mexican
War and he also served in the Civil War. After the Civil War,
the family moved to Knoxville, Tennessee, where Adolph received
most of his education.

While still in school in Knoxville, he began delivering and selling papers. Later, for a short time, he was "cash boy" in the store
of an uncle in Providence, Rhode Island, while he was attending
business school at night. In Knoxville again, he worked for part
of a year as apprentice to a druggist. He registered briefly in the
"primary grade" of East Tennessee University. But these were
brief excursions into another world. At fourteen he was back in
his own world, printer's devil in the shop of the Knoxville
Chronicle.

A little later he decided to go to California, but his way led
through Louisville where he was offered work as compositor on
the *Courier-Journal*. There he remained for two years. In 1877
he moved to Chattanooga where he helped establish the *Dispatch*.
But things didn't go well there and he found himself out of work.

It was right here that his instinct for selling printer's ink first
showed itself in an unusual way. He busied himself publishing
a directory of the city of Chattanooga. He carried through this
difficult and exacting task so well that he made money and established himself as a responsible citizen. So, young as he was, he
was chosen as receiver for the defunct *Chattanooga Times*.

In this paper he saw hope for the future, and with money from his directory he purchased a half-interest in it for only $250. He became its publisher, editor, and business manager. Within an amazingly short time, he had made it not only the leading paper in Chattanooga but one of the leading papers of the entire South. Although he had purchased a half-interest for almost nothing, within less than two years the other half-interest cost him $7,500.

His experience and success in Chattanooga prepared him for his greater effectiveness to the whole country and the world at large. From this small southern city he moved to New York in 1896, the same year that Hearst came to New York from California. He acquired a controlling interest in the *New York Times*.

Now the *Times* was a paper with a great history, but you can't pay dividends on history. This was the point where Mr. Ochs' philosophy of journalism began to show itself. A newspaper was a business enterprise. It had news to sell to the readers and advertising (or rather, blank white space for advertising) to sell to the stores. Now selling advertising to the stores depended upon circulation, and upon nothing else. No matter how much the store owners personally might be in favor of the policy of the paper, they would not buy space on its pages unless it could show a large circulation that would assure them of many readers for their advertising.

At this time the other papers of the city were engaged in a desperate struggle for circulation. Nothing was sacred as they piled one sensation upon another. Headlines screamed at the passer-by. Intimate details of scandals and of private lives were exploited for all they were worth to boost circulation.

Mr. Ochs was just as anxious for circulation as any newspaper man. He was more desperately in need of it than most. The circulation of the *Times* was down to a mere 10,000. Its printing plant was so worn out that it was little better than junk, which was why he had been able to gain a controlling interest in it for a very little money. To its resuscitation he applied the same genius that had raised the Chattanooga *Times* from the grave of debt.

But there was a decided difference in his methods and those of his rivals. Although he accepted frankly the idea of a newspaper as a commercial enterprise rather than a variety of public trust, he took as his motto, "All the news that's fit to print." Through the years this motto has been more restrictive than inclusive. It has meant that the *Times* kept out of its columns the merely sensational and the scandalous. It depended upon news; and news was what it had for sale to the reading customers.

With this in mind, Adolph Ochs set about securing the finest possible product to put on sale. He had already organized the "Southern Associated Press." He also became very active in the affairs of the "Associated Press," of which he was a director from 1900 until his death in 1935. He sent reporters all over the world and maintained correspondents in every center of world affairs. He also provided a coverage for local and national events which put the *Times* in the forefront of reliability.

While perfecting his news-gathering facilities, Ochs steadily refused to include any of the circulation boosters used almost universally by his competitors. There has never been a comic strip in the *Times*. Doubtless comics might have increased the circulation, at least temporarily, but Ochs' faith in news as his merchandise seems to have been justified by the events. There have never been any of the columns of "gossip" or of "advice to the lovelorn," such as are so common in other papers. He made the *Times* a real "news" paper and kept strictly to his own type of merchandise.

He wouldn't tear up the front page with scare headlines that ultimately meant nothing because they were always there. The dignified face of the *Times* has changed little in general appearance since he set its tone. And those papers which seemed to be so successful when the *Times* was struggling for life have, in many cases, retired from the fight. But the *Times* has gone steadily forward.

Ochs was the first publisher to include a section of rotogravure pictures as a part of his Sunday edition. This was in 1914. He was the first to include authoritative news of books in a supplement which is still one of the most popular sections of the Sunday *Times*. His magazine section, bringing feature stories on matters of general importance, has been a criterion of literary and factual value which no one else has been able to duplicate. The *Times* was the first paper to gather news by means of radio, then called "wireless."

It will be seen that these innovations, in contrast to those of his competitors, were all improvements on the primary article of his merchandise—news. The results are eloquent.

In 1934, the last full year of his management, the circulation of the *Times* had increased from the 10,000 it had when he took it over to 466,000 daily and 730,000 Sunday. The advertising was up from a low of two million agate lines per year when he took charge to 20 million in 1934. So successful had he been in selling the white space of his paper that, although it cost him twelve cents to produce each copy, he was able to sell it for 2¢; paying the rest of the cost and a handsome profit from the income of advertising.

In 1905 he built the "Times Building" where Broadway and Seventh Avenue cross. That important center of entertainment and business life has long been called "Times Square," in honor of the building and its builder. The *Times* has become the "newspaper of record" of the United States. An edition is printed regularly on rag paper for preservation by libraries and others interested in keeping a permanent record of events; the index of its news is accepted as the outline of current history.

The methods of the *Times* have been imitated by some of the most successful papers in the country, notably by the Chicago *Daily News,* under Victor Lawson, and the Kansas City *Star,* under William R. Nelson. These, and others in the tradition of the *Times,* have maintained excellent news sources at home and abroad, a dignified front page, and a general avoidance of scandal in reporting the news.

The debt of American journalism to Adolph Ochs is tremendous. It increases, not only as his standards are maintained by the paper with which he was so completely identified for so long, but all over the country as his faith in the innate decency of the common people is justified. It is certainly a worthy tribute to democracy that this faith in people has been justified by the success of the man who dared to maintain it, even though his success is counted in terms of circulation and profits.

The world at large was generous in its recognition of Adolph Ochs. First he was made an honorary Master of Arts by Yale in 1922. Such honors were not as general then as now, but New York University, Dartmouth, Lincoln University and others followed rapidly with doctor's degrees for the man who had never been educated in a college. It was another testimony to the strength of democracy that its educational institutions recognized the worth of a man entirely apart from his possession of the formal testimonials to mental discipline.

He was given the cross of the French Legion of Honor, the Gold Medal of the National Institute of Social Sciences, and innumerable other honorable recognitions. But the one honor which pleased him most was one which a man less deeply devoted to the principles of democracy might easily have overlooked. In 1928 he was made "Citizen Emeritus of the City of Chattanooga," the city in which he had made his first outstanding success and which had prepared him so well for the larger responsibilities of the great metropolis. To be thus honored by those who knew him best (knew him as he could never be known by his fellow citizens of the great city) was, he rightly judged, the finest tribute to his value as a man.

It was also one more tribute to the values of American democracy, since this honor, bestowed upon him by a community made up mainly of Protestant Christian people, was made without reference or consideration of the fact that he was himself a Jew.

The world is indebted to Adolph Ochs, not only because of his contributions to journalism as such, but for his support and encouragement as a journalist to other enterprising pioneers. He did not consider it outside the range of his news interests to give encouragement and financial help to such enterprises as the polar expeditions of Peary, Amundsen, and Byrd. He encouraged Lindbergh in his flights. He was not narrowly nationalistic in this either, for he also supported Scott and Shackelton. His contribution of a half million dollars for the preparation of the manuscripts made possible the printing of the *Dictionary of American Biography* by the Learned Societies of America.

It is well understood that the *Times* is what is called a "conservative" newspaper. It is conservative not only in the make-up of the front page and the suppression of news of a sensational nature, as we have noticed, but it is also conservative in the sense of desiring to maintain things exactly as they are in the social and economic fields. There have been many who have supposed that Adolph Ochs should be held largely responsible for this trend in American journalism, but this is foolish. The papers are conservative not because Ochs or any other man or group of men were conservative. They are conservative because they are a business enterprise. Whereas the original guarantees of a "free press" were intended to protect papers from government control, the control of the press is now, inevitably, in the hands of those who support the press through advertising. The big advertisers are the successful advertisers. The successful advertisers think that conditions as they are, in matters of taxes, wages, hours of work, security, and so on, are pretty good for they are the conditions under which they have succeeded. Therefore, others should be able to succeed under the same conditions. No paper could advocate anything very radically different from what we now have and expect to keep its advertisers.

So this is a trend with which Ochs had little to do. He was, probably, only dimly conscious of the ultimate consequences of making a newspaper a strictly commercial enterprise. In any event, he saved us from a very low form of journalistic exploitation; he held up an estimate of democracy and the common people of a democracy which was in danger of being lost. It is upon such men that we must depend for the solution of the problems of the future, grave as they are. For the wisest and best servants of democracy, in their solution of the problems which they immediately face, are able only to open up the new problems which must be faced and solved by succeeding generations.

So democracy honors herself when she gives honor to the man who started as a printer's devil and rose to provide the world with a living demonstration of the truth of his trust in the profound decency of common folks.

Questions

1. Compare Ochs and Hearst in their influence upon American destiny. Which will have the more permanent effect?

2. Secure a copy of the daily and a copy of the Sunday *Times;* compare it with other newspapers with which you are familiar, in typography, in proportions of news space given to foreign, domestic, local, sports, and other news classifications. Which do you prefer? Which seems to you to serve best the interests of democracy?

3. Secure a copy of *PM,* the New York paper which prints no paid advertisements. Compare it with the *Times.* What are the differences? Do any of these occur because of the difference in advertising policy? May this be the field of the future conflict as decency was the field of battle in the days of Adolph Ochs?

4. Did Ochs need training in a school of journalism? Why not? Why wouldn't the same reasoning hold today, or would it?

Lillian Wald

Crusading Nurse

by

HAROLD B. HUNTING

See! In the rocks of the world
Marches the host of mankind,
A feeble, wavering line.
Where are they tending? A God
Marshalled them, gave them their goal.
Ah, but the way is so long.

Then, in such hour of need
Of your fainting, dispirited race,
Ye, like angels appear,
Radiant with ardor divine.

Order, courage, return;
Eyes rekindling, and prayers
Follow your steps as ye go.
Ye fill up the gaps in our files,
Strengthen the wavering line,
Stablish, continue our march,
On the bound of the waste,
On, to the City of God.

—MATTHEW ARNOLD

ONE COLD MORNING, in March, 1893, a young nurse was giving a talk on the care of the sick to a group of East Side mothers, in New York City. When she had finished, a little girl came up and said that *her* mother was sick and there was nobody to take care of her. They picked their way along dirty streets, the nurse and the child, past vile-smelling uncovered garbage cans, to a tenement house on Ludlow Street. Upstairs, in a

10

two-room rear apartment, she found a family of seven persons. There were boarders, in addition. Most of them slept on the floor. The only bed was occupied by the child's mother, who was dangerously ill. They had not sent for a physician, because there was no money with which to pay him. The sheets on the bed were foul from hemorrhages. The nurse, whose name was Lillian Wald, at once sent for her own physician. Then she bathed the sick woman, changed the sheets, and mopped the floor. When she finally said good-by, and started down the dark, rickety tenement stairs, the family crowded around to kiss her hands.

That morning on Ludlow Street changed the course of Miss Wald's life. She was a graduate nurse and had begun to study in a school of medicine, intending to become a physician, but she never went back to her classrooms and laboratory. All that night she lay awake and, when morning dawned, a new plan had taken shape in her mind: she would find an apartment on the East Side, somewhere near Ludlow Street, where she would live among those poor people and nurse the sick. They would pay when they were able, she knew, and for the rest of her living expenses she would go to those who could afford to help. She would tell the world about the dreadful poverty which she had seen (and smelled) in the midst of the nation's richest city. Surely, she thought, if only people knew about them, such conditions would not be permitted. A few weeks later, Lillian Wald, with her friend and fellow nurse, Mary Brewster, rented the top floor of a house at 27 Jefferson Street, and let it be known in the neighborhood that they were nurses. Although nothing was said about it in the newspapers, few more important events ever occurred in New York.

A Crusader who Searched for Fundamental Causes

Miss Wald was the daughter of Max D. Wald, a well-to-do dealer in optical goods, in Rochester, New York. In this Jewish family, books and music were loved, and there was instant sympathy for all human suffering and need. Lillian's mother, Minnie Wald, never could bear to turn even a hungry tramp from her door. From her, perhaps, came the humanitarian impulse which led Miss Wald into the profession of nursing. From her father, on the other hand, she inherited the scientific turn of mind which searches, coolly and objectively, for underlying causes and which made the work of a nurse congenial to her. For doctors and nurses always look for the causes of disease. They know that it is worse than useless to dose a patient with aconite to bring down his fever, unless they first discover and remove the cause of the fever—the germs of diphtheria, for example, in his system. But Lillian Wald was unique in that she carried this principle to its logical conclusion. She realized that among the causes of disease must be included, not merely disease germs, but also ignorance, overwork, poverty, and corrupt politics. The whole story of her life might be summed up in this way: that she set out to be a nurse; and, in the search for the causes of disease, became the founder of a world-famous social settlement, a leader in a very important modern reform.

She had no idea of becoming a reformer, when she began. But she couldn't be satisfied until she had got at *causes*. Most doctors realize that it is futile to prescribe rest and plenty of good food for a sick man who is too poor to afford either. But the doctor usually feels obliged to shrug his shoulders and say: "What can I do about it?" But Lillian Wald couldn't stop there. "Find out what needs to be done, and find some way to get it done"—that was the rule she lived by. To remove those more far-reaching causes of disease was an "impossible" undertaking, so it seemed. But as some friend once said of her: "Miss Wald cannot believe that she has not strength enough to tackle the universe." In order to make it possible for her East Side friends to get well, she made it her business to nurse back into moral and social health the whole city, the whole nation, the whole world.

THE "NURSES' SETTLEMENT"

When Miss Wald and Miss Brewster went to look for rooms near Ludlow Street, neither of the two had ever heard of a social settlement. At that time there were not many such institutions in existence. Jane Addams had only just begun her work at Hull House in Chicago. They were destined to become close friends, but in those early days neither of them had heard the name of the other. At first, the two young women at 27 Jefferson Street were nurses, and only nurses. But soon they found themselves doing other things besides nursing. They organized mothers' clubs in order to teach them how to care for their children's health. Then came boys' and girls' clubs, through which children could learn the principles of good health in body and mind. By and by there was no longer room at 27 Jefferson Street for all the activities that were going on from day to day, and Miss Wald moved to a new home at 265 Henry Street. (By this time Miss Brewster was married, and no longer with her.) And people in the neighborhood, as well as elsewhere in the city were talking about the "Nurses' Settlement," meaning the work and the institution which had grown up around Lillian Wald. There were objections, however, to this name, "Nurses' Settlement." When athletic teams from the clubs of boys went to play with rival teams, they were frequently greeted with what the boys regarded as insulting jeers, "Noices! Noices!" For that reason, among others, the name of the institution was changed to the "Henry Street Settlement," and the Henry Street Settlement it has remained.

VISITING NURSES AND PUBLIC HEALTH

Neither Miss Wald, nor the Henry Street Settlement, ever lost their special interest in nursing, and out of this interest sprang the organized profession of the visiting nurse, or the public health nurse, that is, the nurse who undertakes to do just what Miss Wald and her friend undertook to do when they went to live on the East Side; the nurse who, in the course of the day's work, goes from one home to another where there are patients to be cared for. She does as much as she can to make the patient comfortable and to fight the disease, in perhaps a half-hour's visit, but her most important work is to show the wife or the mother what needs to be done, and how to do it.

Miss Wald was not the only originator of the idea, for before she began her work, there were visiting nurses already in certain cities, working in connection with church missions and similar institutions. But Miss Wald became the chief sponsor of the idea, and its best embodiment. She did as much or more than anyone else to educate the people of America to the need for this work. Her argument ran somewhat as follows: Most sick persons cannot be sent to hospitals, but must be cared for at home. Indeed, in many instances they are better off at home. Too often the family is poorly equipped for a struggle with serious illness. They should be helped to help themselves; not merely because we are sorry for them, but because sooner or later, uncared-for illness means a bill which all of us must pay. Here, for example, is Mr. Kaplan, with a family of five. His wages are small but, so long as he keeps his health, they can manage to get along. One day Mr. Kaplan comes home with a fever. An epidemic of the flu is going through the factory. Will he lose his job? Not if he can return to his bench within a few days or a week. But suppose the flu develops into pneumonia and the man is unable to work for two months? He loses his job and the family goes "on relief." Would it not have been cheaper for the city to pay the salary of a visiting nurse who would have gone into that home and instructed Mrs. Kaplan in the care of people who have the flu?

The Henry Street Settlement became the headquarters of New York visiting nurses. By 1898 Miss Wald's staff of nurses had increased to nine. In the year 1936, there were 265 nurses going out every morning from this institution to make their rounds; and there were visiting nurse associations in every important American city. During all these years, Miss Wald slept every night like a fireman, with a telephone beside her bed, and personally handled all emergency night calls. Dr. Welch of Johns Hopkins once said that America has made three major contributions to the health of the world. One of these was the Red Cross. Another was the sanitation of the Canal Zone in Panama under Doctor Gorgas. The third contribution was the public-health nurse—and the rapid development of this idea was largely the work of Lillian Wald.

THE SCHOOL NURSE

From the general public health nurse, it was only a short step to the school nurse. There had been school doctors before there were school nurses. People were quick to realize that by having a physician make regular visits to the schools, dangerous epidemics might be checked before getting fairly started. But consider the story of Louis and his bad head. He was twelve years old, and could not read or write. His mother was in despair. "Every time I send him to school," she explained, "the teacher send him home on account of his sore head." No one had ever taken the time and trouble to explain to that mother how to cure Louis' head, and the poor lad was soon to be launched into the struggle of life, handicapped; while the precious years during which he should have been gaining an education were being wasted. But following Miss Wald's talk with the mother, there were two or three regular treatments by one of the Henry Street nurses, and several more by the mother, after she had been told how to apply the necessary ointment. Then one day Louis came dashing up the steps to the Henry Street door: "Look, Miss Wald," he cried, *"I can read!"*

"Why don't we have regularly appointed school nurses," thought Miss Wald, "partly to help the school doctor to detect the earliest symptoms of contagious disease, and to send the sick children home, thereby protecting the others from infection; but even more, to visit the homes of those who have diseases of any kind, and help them to be cured so they can go back to school?" The Board of Education agreed to try the plan in one of the East Side schools, and Miss Lina Rogers of the Henry Street staff was appointed as the first school nurse. During her first month, she made 893 examinations and treatments, and 137 visits to the homes of sick school children. She was able to send back to school 25 children who had been sent home on account of illness but whose cases had not been followed up. Miss Rogers was kept on the job. Today there are nurses at work in almost all American schools, not only in the cities, but even in many country districts.

THE CHILDREN'S BUREAU

Anyone who is interested in health will be interested in the welfare of children. If all children could be kept well, there would be less sickness among adults. One morning Miss Wald was eating breakfast with Mrs. Josephine Kelley, her good friend and fellow resident at Henry Street. They were reading the morning paper while they drank their coffee, and making their own comments on the news items. That morning there was a story to the effect that Congress was about to appropriate several hundred thousand dollars to fight the boll weevil, the little bug which was destroying the cotton crop in Texas. The two women looked at each other, their eyes flashing with the same new idea. "If," they said, "the Federal government can take such an interest in cotton, or in pigs, or wheat, why not in children?"

"Anybody," they said, "can drop a postcard to Washington, any day in the week, and find out how much cotton was raised last year, or how many pigs were shipped abroad. The information will be sent back by return mail—full information in a printed circular. But who knows how many children were born last year in America? Who knows how many died? Who knows how many children under twelve were arrested and sent to prison? Nobody. Why not have a Children's Bureau, to dig up all this information and a vast amount of other information, equally or more important, and make it available to all persons who are endeavoring to make children's lives healthier and happier?"

Through a mutual friend, the idea was passed on to President Theodore Roosevelt, who immediately took it up and persuaded a congressman to introduce a bill proposing to establish such a bureau as Miss Wald and Mrs. Kelley had in mind. It failed of passage—no one seemed to know why. Perhaps there were certain persons with political influence, who profited from the labor of children, and who therefore did not want the bill to become law. Eventually, however, in the administration of President Taft, the bill was passed, and a friend of Lillian Wald, Miss Julia Lathrop, became the first head of the Children's Bureau. This, ever since, has been a storehouse and armory of knowledge for all those who have fought to protect little children from exploitation and oppression.

HELPING THE LABOR UNIONS

Leonora O'Reilly's mother worked in a glove factory. One day she came to Henry Street for advice. The workers in the factory had decided to go out on strike. They had asked for higher wages and the manager had refused. But why should Miss Wald, a nurse,

concern herself about labor unions and strikes? Her answer was
again, that poverty is one of the chief causes of sickness, and the
only way in which hired workers can safeguard themselves from
greedy employers is through unions and collective bargaining.

It happened in this case that the chief owner of this glove factory lived in the same New Jersey suburb with Miss Wald's friend
and backer, John Crosby Brown. Within an hour she was on the
ferry to New Jersey and the next morning the strike was settled
to the satisfaction of all concerned.

Miss Wald was much criticized for letting labor unions hold
meetings in the House on Henry Street. Many a wealthy contributor stopped contributing. Once she was out driving with a
wealthy friend and, passing through a part of the city where there
was a strike going on, they saw one of the union pickets throw a
stone through a factory window. "That's the sort of thing *you*
are encouraging," said her friend.

"I don't like force," replied Miss Wald, "nor unrighteous
strikes, but I have observed that about the only difference between
people in trouble is that rich ones hire lawyers, while the poor ones
throw stones."

THE UNION AGAINST MILITARISM

The first world war broke out in Europe when Lillian Wald was
forty-seven years old; in other words, when she was at the peak
of her success. "War," she said, "is the doom of all that it has
taken years of peace to build up." It was inevitable that the best
energies of the last part of her life should be devoted to the fight
for peace. She saw clearly what so few ever see, that one of the
chief dangers of any war situation is the war hysteria which leads
otherwise peaceful nations to throw themselves into the arms of
their own militarists. She was bitterly opposed to the entrance of
the United States into the war, foreseeing all the evil results
which, ever since the disastrous peace of Versailles, it has been so
easy in retrospect for everybody to see. Late in 1914 an all-day
meeting was held at the Henry Street Settlement, attended by most
of the peace-minded leaders of America. Out of this meeting grew
the American Union Against Militarism.

They were not able to keep America out of the World War, but they did keep us out of war with Mexico—at least they helped greatly. There had been much talk about intervention in the republic to the south of us. "We've got to 'civilize' those Mexicans," people shouted. Then came Villa's raid into Texas, and Pershing's pursuit. At Carrizal, in Mexico, a company of Pershing's men encountered Mexican soldiers and there was shooting. This was described in American newspapers as a treacherous ambush of our troops on the part of the Mexicans. Immediately there was a howl of rage all over America. "We have been patient long enough," said most of our newspapers. "Now let us declare war openly and establish law and order south of the Rio Grande."

But the Union Against Militarism was able to get hold of the truth, which had been suppressed. They published the facts in full-page paid advertisements and appealed to the fair-mindedness of the American people. A conference was held between leading Mexicans and Americans. People on both sides of the boundary began to cool off, and before long, General Pershing's forces were recalled. Later, it was discovered that the Germans, all along, had been trying to embroil the United States in war with Mexico, and that our own hot-headed militarists unconsciously had been playing Germany's game. Would that Miss Wald's counsel could have been followed all through these troubled years!

The Real Lillian Wald

This has been a brief story of some of Miss Wald's great achievements for humanity. But we have yet to make the lady's acquaintance as a real person. Perhaps the best way really to know her is to go down to the East Side and talk with her friends.

Meet this little girl who was making a list of guests to be invited to her birthday party. "Who is this Lillian?" inquired the child's mother. "Is she in your class in school?" "No, she isn't," answered the little girl. "She's been to school. She's Lillian Wald."

Or meet this Chinese laundryman who used to call her, "Heavenly Lady, Number One!" Or this young Negro who said to her, "You've been just like a mother to me, Miss Wald."

Or suppose we talk with those fish peddlers who were in trouble with the police. The mayor had appointed a pushcart commission, and as a result, a misunderstanding had arisen as to what these pushcart men with their fish could do, and what they were not allowed to do. One day, while Miss Wald was entertaining a group of uptown friends at dinner, a delegation of fish peddlers came to the Settlement to ask her advice, whereupon she begged her friends to excuse her from the dinner table. One of the guests asked if he might be allowed to be present at the interview with the fish men, but they refused to permit it. They wanted to be alone with their friend, Miss Wald. "We can talk to *you,* Miss Wald," they explained. "You're just as good as a fish peddler. At least you can *feel* like a fish peddler."

Finally, along with little girls and Chinese laundrymen and fish peddlers and all sorts of other common folk, let us hear from Professor Albert Einstein, often called the world's greatest living scientist. He came to see her at her country home in Westport, Connecticut, not long before her death, and they had a long and delightful talk together. When he rose to go, he said, "I want to thank you, Miss Wald, for your smile." Thousands of men, women and little children have thanked God for Lillian Wald's smile.

Questions for Discussion

1. How far should members of the healing professions carry the principle of search for causes? For example, the leaders of the American Medical Association are bitterly opposed to health co-operatives—yet millions of our people, because of poverty, cannot afford proper medical care. What do you think about socialized medicine?

2. One of Miss Wald's nurses visited a home where a baby was being born. A private doctor had been called and he had left the mother to suffer, uncared for, because there was no money in the house to pay him. The nurse reported him to his local medical association, but nothing was done to rebuke him, because the nurse had violated professional ethics in taking action against him. What changes would you advocate in the ethics of the nurses' profession?

3. Miss Wald was very reticent about her religious beliefs and emotions. But from her life story would you call her a religious person? Why?

4. Was Miss Wald justified in her fear of our own American militarism? Is it not necessary that the United States should be prepared to defend itself?

Projects

1. If you live in New York, or if you ever go to New York, visit the Henry Street Settlement.

2. Find out whether there is a Visiting Nurses' Association in your city or county. What does it do?

Books by and about Miss Wald

Lillian Wald, *The House on Henry Street*. Henry Holt and Company, New York, 1915.

————, *Windows on Henry Street*. (A sequel to the above, written about twenty years later.) Little, Brown & Co., Boston, 1933.

R. L. Duffus, *Lillian Wald, Neighbor and Crusader*. The Macmillan Co., New York, 1938.

Charney Vladeck

A Revolutionist Devoid of Hate

by

HAROLD B. HUNTING

"We are the workers and makers!
We are no longer dumb!
Tremble, O shirkers and takers,
Sweeping the earth, we come."

—JOHN G. NEIHARDT

O<small>N</small> THANKSGIVING DAY, in the year 1908, a young immigrant, twenty-three years old, landed from his steamer at
Ellis Island, New York Harbor. He carried a basket, and
the basket was wrapped in a shawl to conceal the fact that it was
empty. He did not want people to know that he had absolutely no
possessions. If he had not had friends in this country, doubtless the
authorities would not have admitted him to the United States, but
his friends stood sponsor for him that he would not become a public charge. His name was Charney Vladeck.

When he died, thirty years later, more than half a million people crowded into the streets of New York to do him honor as his
funeral procession passed. Mostly they were poor people, working
people. They loved him because he had been one of their ablest
and most fearless champions in the struggle against oppression.
Yet there were others, not poor, who honored him for his fair-
mindedness and unselfishness. Mr. Oswald Garrison Villard, the
journalist, said of him: "I never heard from his lips one word
that was other than unselfish and fine." Mayor La Guardia of
New York City said (referring to that struggle against oppression): "Charney, we will carry on!" It was well for America that

21

she admitted that young Jew to her shores. He gave to his adopted country as much as he received, and a little more. His basket may have been empty that day, but his mind was not empty of ideas, nor his heart of sympathy for his fellow men.

BOYHOOD DAYS

Charney Vladeck was born in the village of Dookorah, near the city of Minsk, in northwest Russia. Charney was the family name, and the boy was christened Baruch. Vladeck came later, as we shall see. When he was only two years old his father died, leaving his mother with a large family to support by keeping a small leather supply store. "We lived on baked potatoes and cereals, and the Talmud and the Hebrew prophets," wrote her son, years afterward. But, like all Hebrew mothers, she was determined that her children should receive an education, no matter what the cost in money and hardship. Baruch and his brother Samuel went to the village synagogue school where they showed such promise of ability that their teacher urged them to go farther. So the two boys were sent to the school in Minsk where young men were trained to be rabbis. To become a rabbi was the highest honor that any lad could aspire to. Gladly they set off to the big city and, having almost no money at all, they found a tiny room with single bed, where night after night they took turns sleeping on the floor. According to an old Jewish custom, the board of students who were to be rabbis was supposed to be furnished by the members of the synagogue. So the two boys went each day for their meals to a different house, sometimes walking many miles, sometimes eating leftovers with the servants in the kitchen, though at other times they were given an honored place at the family dinner table. At any rate they managed to live and they studied—mostly the Talmud and the Old Testament in the orignal Hebrew. The young Baruch also found time to peep inside the covers of other books. Before long he was devouring the contents of the great Russian classics, Tolstoy, Turgenev, Dostoievski, and the rest. He began to try his hand at writing short stories and poems of his own. As his audiences in America were to discover, he had the spark of genius in his mind and heart, and might easily have won for himself an honored name in the world of literature, except that his sympathies drew him to people even more than to books. He was destined to spend his life fighting for liberty, rather than writing books about it.

BECOMING A REVOLUTIONIST

Already, in Minsk, whispers were going about regarding secret meetings which were being held in the woods out beyond the city limits. The son of one of the local rabbis had disappeared and it was rumored that he had been exiled to Siberia. Little by little, young Charney was drawn into this revolutionary movement. He conducted classes for young workingmen in literature and economics, and in 1904, when he was eighteen years old, he was arrested for this and thrown into jail. His year in jail only gave him a chance to read more books and to meet other political prisoners and learn from them. In those days it used to be said that the prisons were the universities of the people. The revolutionaries even looked forward to a term in prison now and then, as a chance to catch up on their reading.

During this first jail term of Charney's, it happened one day that news drifted in from outside, about the death of Von Plehve. This man was one of the most detestable of all the Czarist officials, persecuting without mercy, and murdering Jews, labor leaders, and even the most moderate reformers. Charney never believed in assassination as a way of getting rid of tyrants, but neither he nor any of his fellow prisoners could help rejoicing at the death of this miserable monster, and they determined to celebrate. They knew that every evening the prison warden was in the habit of locking the doors of the building from the outside and then going forth to parts unknown. When night came on the officer, as usual, locked up and went off. Immediately, in every cell of the prison, on the side towards the city, the prisoners stuffed their filthy straw mattresses against the barred cell windows, and, at a given signal, set them afire. The illumination was seen throughout the city. The police and the soldiers came running, but could not open the locked door. Not until hours later did the warden return with the key, but by then there was nothing to be done. The stone cells

were, of course, fire-proof and, incidentally, perhaps much cleaner
and less vermin-ridden because of the blaze.

PLAYING HIDE AND SEEK WITH THE CZARIST POLICE

Baruch Charney came out of that first term in the Minsk prison
a convinced revolutionist. The old system was so obviously rotten
to the core that he was determined to give his life to its overthrow
and to the building of a new and free Russia. The next four years
were spent going from town to town, organizing the workers and
peasants and urging them to be ready, when the opportunity should
come, to strike a blow for freedom. Most of the time he had to
travel under an assumed name, lest the police should discover and
arrest him. Vladeck was one of the aliases which he used; it happened to stick with his friends, as well as his enemies, so that
Baruch Charney came to be known as Charney Vladeck. Twice
he was caught and sent to prison. While serving one of these
prison terms, he and his fellow prisoners went on a hunger strike
to protest against some piece of tyranny, and the strike was successful. Their protest was heeded.

In the winter of 1905 the terrible massacre of the peasants took
place in front of the palace of the Czar. These simple folk had
believed that if only they could bring their wrongs to the attention
of the great white father, the Czar himself, he would see that
justice was done. They were led by a sympathetic priest, Father
Gapon, and came, with their petition, to the great square in front
of the Winter Palace. But there they were shot down, hundreds
of them, by the Czar's own order, with bullets from the guns of
his personal bodyguard. A wave of indignation swept over Russia
and over the world. Vladeck, at this time, was out of prison and
in Minsk. When news of the massacre came, he went to the city
steel mill and shouted to the men to come out on strike. Now may
be the time, he thought, for the decisive blow. Out came the men,
singing and cheering. Then somebody shouted: "Look out! The
Cossacks!" In a moment these mounted soldiers were riding the
workers down under the hoofs of their horses, clubbing and cutting everybody within reach of their sabres. Vladeck was struck
down in the snow, and lay bleeding and unconscious for hours.

In the darkness of the early winter night, he crept to the house of a friendly family and then, lest he involve them in trouble, fled to another town. To the end of his life he bore on his face the white scar from that Cossack sword. To the end of his life, also, the terror of those experiences haunted his dreams.

Conditions in Russia gradually grew more and more intolerable. Thousands of young Russian idealists were being shipped off to Siberia, to be buried alive, as it were, in those frozen wastes. Vladeck's own steps were being dogged more persistently and cunningly. It became apparent that he could do little there for the cause of freedom, since only a few dared to come near him or to be found with him. Almost any day he was doomed to feel on his arm the heavy hand of the police or of some Cossack soldier. He determined to escape from Russia to America. So it came about that he landed in New York that Thanksgiving Day.

AMERICA, THE PROMISED LAND

Like many another exile from European despotism, the young Vladeck was entranced by "America the Beautiful." He loved her better, or at least more intelligently, than many a native son. He loved the beauty of her "waving fields of grain" and of her "purple mountain majesties." Within a few weeks after his arrival he set forth on a lecture tour which took him to many cities in the United States and in Canada. Thus he was able to see Yellowstone Park and the Grand Canyon of the Colorado; and he wrote glorious descriptions of his experiences. He also loved America for its human freedom. Everywhere he found people treating each other as equals. There was no caste system, no cringing and fawning before lords and dukes, no cruel flogging of helpless peasants and workers. As compared with Russia, this was in truth the land of the free, a veritable land of promise, and he was eager to become a naturalized citizen. He took out his first and second citizenship papers as soon as the law permitted. And on the election day when he went to the polls to cast his first vote, he wore his best clothes, just as though it were the Sabbath Day and he were going to the synagogue to worship God.

INJUSTICES EVEN IN AMERICA

In his travels, however, Vladeck saw other sides of American life which were not so beautiful as the sunlight on the walls of the Grand Canyon. In one southern city he saw the police raiding the Negro quarter, beating up its inhabitants with their clubs, although most of them certainly were innocent of crime. When he went to the police chief and protested, that officer said to him: "If you fellows don't like this country, you can go back where you came from." In another locality, he again saw Negroes being beaten, this time by drunken sailors. When he spoke about this to friends of his, they merely smiled. "You are a greenhorn," they said. "You will learn better than to let these things disturb you."

In one city where he was visiting, it happened that there was a strike of the motormen and conductors on the street railway system. They wanted higher wages, or shorter hours. Vladeck was walking down the main street, where many of the strikers had gathered, when a squad of police came running around the corner, swinging their clubs. Once again, Vladeck was knocked to the sidewalk, though he was only an onlooker this time, an "innocent bystander." Was this a city in the land of brotherhood or was it Minsk? Was he in America or back in Russia?

Even that first vote which he had cast with such solemn pride was never counted. He learned afterward that the boss of the election district had boasted that all ballots which were not "right" were thrown into the furnace.

A CRUSADER FOR DEMOCRACY

Charney Vladeck was a Socialist; meaning by that word, not an advocate of a dictatorship like that which has developed in Russia under the Soviet rulers, but rather a democracy of all workers, whether workers with hand or with brain. His dream was "the American dream," namely, equal opportunity for all men. He wanted to set free the millions of factory workers who were in continual fear of a cut in wages, or of discharge and unemployment. He wanted the farmer to escape from between the upper and lower millstones, on the one hand the bank or mortgage company which might foreclose when he could not pay the interest on their loan, and on the other hand the big monopolies which forced down the prices which he received for his products, the milk distributors, the millers, the meat packers, and so on. He wanted for all of us a government uncorrupted by selfish special interests. He found an excellent weapon ready for his use in this crusade. It was the great Jewish daily newspaper, *Forward,* of which he was made city editor, in 1916. This paper had for years been fighting on behalf of the Amalgamated Clothing Workers of America, the International Ladies' Garment Workers, and many other unions, in their struggle to bargain collectively with powerful employers and employers' associations for fair wages and working conditions. Mr. Vladeck poured into *Forward* all the resources of his heart and brain.

About the same time, he began to take an active part in New York City politics. He campaigned in 1916 for Meyer London, who was elected to the Congress of the United States from a New York City district. In 1917, he himself was nominated on the Socialist ticket for the city Board of Aldermen and, with six other Socialists, was elected. In spite of bitter attacks because of his reform program, he was re-elected for a second term. From that time on there was scarcely a single forward-looking movement in New York in which he did not play a part. He became one of the directors of the Amalgamated Co-operative Houses in the Bronx and in Brooklyn, through which low-cost comfortable apartments were provided for familes of workingmen with low incomes. In 1934, he was appointed by Mayor La Guardia to the New York Housing Authority, through which, in co-operation with the Federal Government, block after block of new, well-lighted and heated apartment houses took the place of miserable slums.

DEBATES IN THE CITY COUNCIL

Under the new city charter, Mr. Vladeck was elected to the New York City Council in 1936, and he became the minority leader in that body. This position gave him a new vantage ground from which to fight for the cause of human rights. Largely because of his aggressive advocacy of measures which some considered radical, the sessions of the Council were usualy crowded with private citizens who were eager to listen to the debates between Mr. Vladeck and his opponents. At almost every meeting there flashed the shining sword blades of clashing arguments and witty rejoinders.

For example there was the debate on proportional representation. Very often, under our present laws, a minority in an election is left with no voice whatever in the government, even though it may have been a numerous minority. Mr. Vladeck believed that more adequate provision should be made for minority representation in the legislature. "Your scheme would not work," said his opponents. "Look at the Bronx, with its enormous Jewish population! Yet its representatives in the legislature are not Jewish. Even though they are in the majority, they cannot get themselves represented."

To which Mr. Vladeck replied, "Intelligent Jews in this community resent the idea of voting as Jews in any election, rather than as American citizens. They resent the idea of voting, not on the basis of the common good, but on the basis of racial or religious affiliations."

Often there was a rich and salty humor in Mr. Vladeck's sallies. At one session a speaker made a nasty fling at the foreign-born members of the Council. Mr. Vladeck himself still spoke with a foreign accent. "*My* grandfather," shouted this speaker, "was a neighbor of Abraham Lincoln. He was a native-born American." "My ancestors," replied Mr. Vladeck, "were neighbors of Moses, and everybody knows that Moses was secretary to God."

At another session Mr. Vladeck was attacked because of his record as a revolutionist in Russia; on the theory that here in this country, just as in Russia, he was trying to overthrow the government. The speaker was an Irishman.

"What were your ancestors doing in Ireland when that country was fighting for its freedom?" cried Vladeck. "Either they were in jail most of the time or they were not good Irishmen!"

The New York City of fifty years ago was a filthy city and a corrupt city. Less than fifty years ago, in New York's Triangle Building fire, a hundred working girls were burned to death or killed on the pavement to which they jumped, because of the greed of employers who sacrificed safety to profits. In comparison, the city of Greater New York is today a miracle of good citizenship and honest government. Its streets are clean. Its great system of parks and beaches provides opportunities for fresh air and recreation, even to the poorest. Its slums are gradually being wiped out. In this transformation, Charney Vladeck played no small part.

A JEW WHO LOVED HUMANITY

One Friday night when Baruch Charney was a little boy, he and his mother were left alone in their cottage, the rest of the family having gone to the synagogue for evening prayer. The mother hugged her boy to her side, and sang to him one of the hymns of their Jewish worship:

> *Around the walls of Jerusalem*
> *Little Jews stand*
> *Weeping and sobbing.*

The boy looked up questioningly. "Mother," he asked, "in the whole world is it only the Jews who stand weeping and sobbing?"

"No, dear child," replied the mother. "It is all the poor and the oppressed."

Charney Vladeck never forgot that all the poor and the oppressed of all races stand weeping, waiting for a leader and a deliverer. His whole life was consecrated to their service.

Questions for Discussion

1. It is sometimes asserted that no privileged group or class has ever yielded to the claims of justice for the oppressed, except through violence, or ever will so yield. Consider Vladeck's career, both in Russia and in the United States. What light does it throw on this problem?

2. Why is it that men and women who come as immigrants to America are so often more passionately loyal to this country than native-born citizens?

3. Why is it that the Jewish race has always produced so large a proportion of idealists, men like Vladeck, warriors for human rights?

Projects

1. If you live in New York or if you ever go to New York, visit the
Vladeck Memorial Housing Center, on the East Side. Inquire about it
at the City Hall.

2. Secure a copy of the Jewish daily *Forward* (at a newsstand, or in
the reading room of your public library, or send five cents to the office
of the *Forward* in New York). Is it still carrying on the fight for justice?

Bibliography

Source materials on Vladeck in published form are very meager. The
author consulted various magazines and had a personal interview with Mrs.
Vladeck and her son and daughter. The Jewish daily *Forward* presented the
author a pamphlet entitled *Baruch Charney Vladeck*, by John Herling. Nothing
is available in book form.

Rabbi Stephen S. Wise

Outstanding American Rabbi

by

IVAN GEROULD GRIMSHAW

A free pulpit, worthily filled, must command respect and influence; a pulpit that is not free, howsoever filled, is sure to be without potency or honor. A free pulpit will sometimes stumble into error; a pulpit that is not free can never powerfully plead for truth and righteousness.—

— STEPHEN S. WISE

"WHEN RABBI WISE attacks a politician, steamship business to Europe improves immediately." These were the words of Mayor LaGuardia of New York City, at the banquet in honor of the sixtieth anniversary of the birth of Rabbi Stephen S. Wise of that city. Back of the jesting words of the mayor was a great truth concerning this man whose prophetic Judaism has flowed into all the interests of his life. No living minister of any faith has more profoundly touched the larger issues of American life. No one has plunged more deeply into the heart of the economic and social problems of our day. Fearless in his attacks upon evil and evil-doers, the rabbi of New York's Free Synagogue has long been a power to be reckoned with wherever social injustices are found.

Who, then, is this man who has been hailed as "the outstanding rabbi in American Jewish history." What were the factors responsible for his ideas and ideals?

HOME BACKGROUND

Rabbi Wise was a son of the manse. He was born in Budapest, Hungary, March 17, 1874, the son of Aaron and Sabine De Fischer

31

Wise. His father's father, the Rev. Joseph H. Wise, had also been
a Hungarian rabbi of note. When Stephen was only a year old he
was brought to the United States by his parents. The family settled
in New York City where the father became minister of Temple
Rodeph Sholem, which position he held until his death in 1896.
Many years afterwards, Dr. Stephen Wise paid high tribute to the
influence of that home. Writing, as he said, "between the fiftieth
and sixtieth longitudinal lines" an article on "Why I Have Found
Life Worth Living," he declared:

I have found life worth living on many grounds: first, because of
what has come to me as an individual—what I call life's Unearned
Increment. No one could have lived in two such homes as I have without finding life abundantly worth living. There was the earlier home
prepared for me as it were out of the past by parents and by their remoter
forbears, who had a goodly part in shaping and coloring my life. That
parental, humbly circumstanced home of a minister's family was rich in
homely and vivid and colorful associations, a goodly-wise mother, a
father, above all else, the gentlest of teachers and the truest of comrades,
brothers and sisters of varying types but all loved.[1]

On the same occasion also he paid high tribute to his father as
the one who had enabled him to see the ministry as a high calling
and a noble cause.

EDUCATION FOR THE RABBINATE

There seems never to have been any question as to the vocational
path which young Wise would follow. After graduating from the
public schools of New York City, Stephen studied at the College
of the City of New York in the years 1887 to 1891, specializing in
classics and languages; he then took courses in Semitics and philosophy at Colombia University, graduating with a B.A. in 1892. Now
began his real training for the rabbinate. Study for the Hebrew
ministry began under the watchful eye of his father. He also had
the tutelage of such great scholars as Prof. Max L. Margolis, Dr.
Alexander Kohut, and Dr. Henry Gersoni.

His first appointment was as assistant to Dr. Henry S. Jacobs of

---
[1] *The Christian Century,* October 11, 1928, Vol. 45, p. 1223.

B'nai Jeshurun Temple in New York City. Within a year he succeeded Dr. Jacobs in that synagogue. In this position he laid the foundation of his subsequent distinction as a reform rabbi in the religious and social progress of American Jewry. It was during this period that he first identified himself with the Zionist movement of which he was in later years to become chairman. During these years also he continued his education, securing the coveted Ph.D. from Columbia University in the year 1901.

FROM EAST TO WEST

In the year 1900 occurred two events important in the life of the young rabbi: He married Louise Waterman, daughter of Julius Waterman of New York City, and also received a call to become rabbi of a synagogue on the other side of the continent.

There is good reason to believe that the young rabbi, when he set out on a trek across the country to a completely new environment and into an unknown territory, had much in common with that most famous of his Semitic ancestors—Abraham, who was commanded: "Get thee out of thy country, and from thy kindred, and from thy father's house, unto the land that I will show thee," (Genesis 12:1) and who, having been called, "obeyed to go out unto a place which he was to receive as an inheritance." (Hebrews 11:8.)

Rabbi Wise would perhaps have been the first to deny the validity of the latter phrase of the quotation from the book of Hebrews, for while he was no doubt honored to be called to the pastorate of Temple Beth Israel in Portland, Oregon, he soon discovered that he had "inherited" many things not much to his liking. To the work of changing this situation he early devoted himself.

He was not content to devote himself exclusively to the building up of his own organization. He had broader interests than that. But let no one think that he shirked that duty. His efforts on behalf of his own synagogue and religious group resulted in his more than doubling his congregation, and in making it conspicuous by its generous contributions to every Jewish cause. His work on behalf of the religious needs of Oregon and the adjacent parts of

Washington and Idaho was limited only by exhaustion resulting from the hardships of travel.

But in addition to all this, he gave himself unstintingly to the work of social service to which he devoted his commanding qualities of culture and eloquence. Hardly had he begun his work in Portland when it was borne in upon his sensitive soul that child labor was one of the evils of that great state. And well might it be, for there was no law whatever on the statute books even so much as to hold the evil practice in check. Just the challenge to be presented to this eager young prophet! With the aid of friends in the East, he succeeded in drafting a law of such high caliber as to place Oregon alongside the leading states in the line of social reform. But child-labor legislation was not his only interest. He found time from his other duties to become one of the founders of the Oregon State Board of Charities and Correction, and its first vice-president. He also labored valiantly for the recognition of the importance of the work of the Juvenile Court, and for such important advances as the instituting of the indeterminate sentence, and the paroling of first offenders. No wonder that an expert authority could say of these things for which Dr. Wise was largely responsible, "At one step Oregon has gone to the front in penal legislation."

Yet with all this he did not ignore the needs of his own city. He was responsible for establishing in the city of Portland "The People's Forum," which had many of the social values of the old New England town meeting. Here, at weekly meetings, all matters of civic interest were brought to a free platform for discussion. This repeatedly proved effective in throttling sinister schemes. Dr. Wise's efficient service as founder and president of the forum brought him an invitation to become one of the members of Portland's Executive Board of Nine, in whom, under the Mayor, the municipal government of that city was vested.

THE PRICE OF FREEDOM

The news of the good work which was being done by this daring reformer spread in ever widening circles. News of it trickled back to his own native New York. Here was a man who could appeal to the crowds. What an asset he would be to a New York synagogue! There were those in New York who were determined to lure him back and in the year 1905 he was invited to preach in Temple Emanu-El, New York's greatest and richest synagogue. It was, in effect, a series of trial sermons by which the trustees might determine whether or not they wanted to recommend him to the congregation as a possible choice for their rabbi.

His sermons were such as to warrant extending a call to him, but in the offer, both written and spoken, there was one clause which drew his attention and elicited a reply which attracted nation-wide attention to Dr. Wise. That condition was that the pulpit of Temple Emanu-El "shall always be subject to, and under the control of the Board of Trustees." When in answer to his frank question concerning the meaning of this condition he was given the equally frank answer that "should the rabbi in his sermons or addresses offend the opinion of the lay heads of the congregation, he would be expected either to retract the offending remarks or to maintain a discreet silence on the subject thereafter," [2] Dr. Wise declined the pulpit in an open letter to the congregation of Temple Emanu-El. It has become a classic utterance in behalf of an unmuzzled pulpit. In this letter he declared:

The chief office of the minister, I take it, is not to represent the views of the congregation, but to proclaim the truth as he sees it. How can he serve a congregation as a teacher save as he quickens the minds of his hearers by the vitality and independence of his utterances? A free pulpit, worthily filled, must command respect and influence; a pulpit that is not free, howsoever filled, is sure to be without potency or honor. A free pulpit will sometimes stumble into error; a pulpit that is not free can never powerfully plead for truth and righteousness. In the pursuit of the duties of his office, the minister may from time to time be under the necessity of giving expression to views at variance with the views of some, or even many, members of the congregation.

Far from such difference proving the pulpit to be in the wrong, it may be, and ofttimes is, found to signify that the pulpit has done its duty in calling evil evil and good good, in abhorring the moral wrong of putting light for darkness and darkness for light, and in scorning to limit itself to the utterance of what the prophet has styled "smooth things," lest variance of views arise. Too great a dread there may be

---

[2] Wise, J. W., *Jews are Like That*, Brentano's, New York, 1928, pp. 87-88.

of secession on the part of some members of a congregation, for, after all, difference and disquiet, even schism at the worst, are not so much to be feared as the attitude of the publit which never provokes dissent because it is cautious rather than courageous, peace-loving rather than prophetic, time-serving rather than right-serving.[3]

This letter, when reprinted in various newspapers, proved a storm center of controversy. Many a conventional rabbi and minister gave thanks that he was not like this young upstart and knew enough to realize that the pulpit should remain the eloquent sounding board for the opinions of the members of the congregation, especially the ones seated in the higher-priced pews. Other men equally fervently admired the rabbi for his courage in doing that which they would much liked to have done but did not dare to do.

As it is often the case, good was forthcoming out of evil. True it was that Dr. Wise had lost his opportunity to become rabbi of the richest synagogue in New York City. Yet there were some daring Jews, many of them men of influence, in whose hearts his fearless insistence upon religious freedom within the synagogue struck a responsive note. Thus it was that in the year 1907 he came back to New York City determined to inaugurate a synagogue movement, "the occupant of whose pulpit should be free to speak the truth even when that truth might be distasteful to the congregation which he served."[4]

A Free Preacher in a Free Pulpit

The Free Synagogue was set up in a building on West 81st Street in what had been a Universalist church. In all the intervening years it has been a "universalist" church—a church for all who do not fear the truth. The main tenets of the organization are briefly stated:

1. No pews and no dues; voluntary contributions and a democratic organization.
2. A free pulpit.
3. The preaching of vital, prophetic Judaism.

---

[3] Ingle, W., "Celebrities at Home," *Harper's Weekly,* December 5, 1908, Vol. 52, p. 13.
[4] Wise, J. W., *op. cit.,* p. 89.

These the founders elaborated in the constitution of the Free Synagogue through such statements as:

Desirous of reasserting a fundamental ideal of Israel, the founders of the Free Synagogue resolve that it shall not at any time nor for any reason impose any pecuniary due, tax, or assessment upon its members, but it shall be supported wholly by voluntary contributions.

Believing that Judaism is a religion of perpetual growth and development, we hold that, while loyal to the fundamental teachings thereof, we are, and by virtue of the genius of Israel ought to be, free to interpret and to restate the teachings of Israel of the past in the light of the present, and that each succeeding generation in Israel is free to reformulate the truths first intrusted in the providence of God to our fathers.

Believing that the power of the synagogue for good depends in part upon the inherent right of the pulpit to freedom of thought and speech, the founders of the Free Synagogue resolve that its pulpit shall be free to preach on behalf of truth and righteousness in the spirit and after the pattern of the prophets of Israel.[5]

Throughout the years Rabbi Wise has continued to serve the Free Synagogue, interpreting most broadly his right to preach "a vital and prophetic Judaism." During all his long and distinguished career he has been a valiant fighter for social justice and political reform; and to his credit are many outstanding achievements in this field. Though often denounced, often accused of playing to the galleries, he is still "the outstanding rabbi of American Jewish history." His contribution is well summed up in the words of a fellow rabbi:

Almost singlehanded [he] has transformed liberal Judaism in America. He found it conventional, smug, fettered and barren. He poured into it his passion for social justice, his intense love of freedom, his devotion to the Jewish masses and their eternal hopes, and gave it life. If today the liberal Jewish pulpit is free, if the rabbis are earnestly concerned with the social and economic implications of their religion, if the reform synagogue has been democratized in form and spirit, if contact with catholic Israel has revitalized the entire liberal Jewish group, it is largely because Stephen S. Wise sounded the tocsin of revolt and courageously led the march to new goals.[6]

---

[5] Ingle, J. W., *op. cit.*, p. 14.
[6] Bernstein, P. S., "Rabbi Wise," *The Christian Century*, May 16, 1934, Vol. 51, p. 666.

For Discussion

1. Dr. Wise has always been much interested in the family. What part do you think his boyhood home had in fostering this interest?

2. Do you feel that a minister has a right to participate actively in politics? What of the old admonition: "Cobbler, stick to thy last?"

3. Do you agree with Dr. Wise's method of sending a letter to be read to the congregation of the church whose offer of the pastorate he would not accept? Was he justified in refusing their offer because he would have been subject to the Board of Trustees?

4. Discuss this statement by Rabbi Wise: "The Church is not to patronize the masses, nor to be patronized by the classes."

5. It is the boast of the leaders of the Free Synagogue that some members contribute as little as five dollars yearly and yet are members on equal standing with those who contribute as much as one thousand dollars annually. Does this arrangement seem fair to you?

6. During the strike of the needle trades, Dr. Wise delivered a stirring attack from the pulpit against the Associated Waist and Dress Manufacturers, many of whose members were in his congregation, for refusing to arbitrate. Some offended listeners threatened to resign from the synagogue, and he enthusiastically invited them to do so. What do you think of his action in this matter?

For Further Reading

Jones, Edgar DeWitt, *American Preachers To-day*, Bobbs-Merrill Company, Indianapolis, 1933, Chap. VI.

Wise, J. W., *Jews Are Like That*, Brentano's, New York, 1928, Chapter on "Stephen S. Wise."

Wise, Stephen S., *Child versus Parent*, Macmillan Company, New York, 1922.

Bernstein, P. S., "Rabbi Wise," *The Christian Century*, May 16, 1934, Vol. 51, p. 666.

Goldberg, B. Z., "Rabbi Wise Stirs Up a Hornet's Nest," *Outlook*, Jan. 13, 1926, Vol. 142, pp. 62-63.

Minsky, L., "Paradoxical Rabbi," *The Christian Century*, April 18, 1934, Vol. 51, pp. 525-527.

Wise, Stephen S., *"Gaudium Certaminis*: Why I Have Found Life Worth Living," *The Christian Century*, October 11, 1928, Vol. 45, pp. 1223-1225.

————, "Life and Teachings of Jesus the Jew," *Outlook*, June 7, 1913, Vol. 104, pp. 295-297.

Charles Proteus Steinmetz

Wizard of Schenectady

by

IVAN GEROULD GRIMSHAW

Measure thy life by loss instead of gain;
Not by the wine drunk, but wine poured forth;
For love's strength standeth in love's sacrifice;
And whoso suffers most hath most to give.

—H. E. H. KING

IF EVER A MAN was given a name untrue to his character, Steinmetz, when he was given the name "Proteus," was that man. For while the fabled sea god Proteus has given us the English adjective *protean,* which is a synonym for variable and inconstant, neither of these adjectives could honestly be applied to the "wizard of Schenectady." In only one way might there be a connection. The fabled sea god had the power of changing himself into an endless variety of forms. There were no doubt times when Charles Steinmetz envied him that power and wished that he might exchange his own poor misshapen body, with its crooked back and twisted leg, for one more normal. Yet on the other hand, while heredity had played him a mean trick in the kind of body provided, she had dealt generously with him in the matter of intellect, so to the improving of that he gave himself ceaselessly.

BIRTH AND EARLY LIFE

The father of Charles Steinmetz was employed as a lithographer at the time of the birth of his son, Karl August Rudolf (it was not until years later that he was dubbed "Proteus" by some of his fellow students). In later years he became an employee of the railroad. A few years previously he had married the widow of his deceased brother and had taken under his protection her two small daughters. At the time that Karl was born, April 9, 1865, the family was occupying a small flat on the Tuenzienstrasse in Breslau, Germany.

The death of the mother from cholera, a year after Karl's birth, strengthened the father's determination to do all in his power to protect this son who had inherited a physical deformity from which he himself had so long suffered, and to bend all his efforts to see to it that his son should be well educated. As a result, after passing through the German elementary schools and the gymnasium, to test fully his tastes and capabilities Karl took preparatory courses in medicine, political economy, mechanical engineering, and other studies at the University of Breslau. Finally, however, he gave himself fully to comprehensive work in mathematics, higher chemistry, and electricity.

Steinmetz spent six years at the University of Breslau but never received its highly coveted degree. For when the time for the giving of the degree came, he found himself an expatriate in Switzerland. There is reason to believe that the honorary M.A. granted to him by Harvard many years later, or the Ph.D. with which Union College honored him, never meant what this undergraduate degree would have. Always gregarious by nature, he quickly associated himself with various student groups. One such group was interested in making evident to the world the meaning of Socialism. "It was not Socialism as generally understood in America today. It was an idealistic creed, rosy-tinted to the mental vision, aspiring unto perfection for human society, and fired with all the enthusiasm of youth."[1] Yet this made it no more acceptable to the German government. Bismarck with his severe policies was then at the helm and socialism was persecuted as something abhorrent to the government and intolerable to the nation.

For four years Steinmetz kept his membership in the group a secret from the police but finally, when he was informed that a

---

[1] Hammond, John Winthrop, *Charles Proteus Steinmetz,* D. Appleton-Century Company, New York, 1935, pp. 72-73.

paper had been sworn out for his arrest, he determined to go, and go quickly. The next morning, gathering up his few belongings (among them his thesis already approved by the professors and about to be printed in the university mathematics journal), he bade goodby to his father and took an early train on the railroad his father had served so humbly and long. As the train moved out of the city on its way to the Austrian frontier, he no doubt smiled wistfully as he watched the Gothic roofs of his native city disappear from his sight forever. Never again was he to see his father who, while not exactly a comrade, had been an interested observer of his activities and progress.

THE LAND OF THE FREE

After but a day or two in Austria, Steinmetz took train for Switzerland, finally landing in the city of Zurich. After considerable difficulty—due to his not being able to obtain a certificate of residence from the authorities in Breslau—he registered in the Zurich Polytechnic School, where he succeeded in securing six months of graduate training. Yet from Zurich he obtained much more than graduate training, for it was in that Swiss city that he met a young Dane named Asmussen, who gave him a vision of a present Utopia—America—almost as inspiring as the Utopia the Socialists proposed.

To young Steinmetz it seemed an unattainable Utopia, for to come to America cost money and of that necessary article he had little. However, when young Asmussen prepared to set out for America upon the command of his uncle in California, he proposed that Steinmetz go with him. Aware of Steinmetz's poverty, he suggested that he could pay the ways of both of them if they were to go steerage. After much discussion Steinmetz was finally persuaded. Forced to avoid travel through Germany, they set out by the way of Cherbourg and Paris, thence going to Havre, where they embarked on a French immigrant steamer *La Champagne*. After eight days of what Steinmetz later referred to as "the most pleasant trip I ever made," they arrived within sight of the land of the free and its guardian, the Statue of Liberty.

EARLY TRIALS OF AN IMMIGRANT

The trials of the new immigrant now began. His earliest view of the new Utopia was to be from behind the bars of the detention pen. On the way over he had sought to learn the English language but had only succeeded in picking up a few scattered phrases. When he faced the immigration authorities he had little to recommend him. As they viewed this deformed young man, forlorn in appearance, with his face swelled from exposure to a cold damp wind through an open port hole, with only a stumbling knowledge of English, and with no money in his pocket, they had no way of realizing that here was the electrical wizard of the future. Hence the decision that he could not land! That he must go back to Europe! Temporarily, to the detention pen.

Again the friendly Dane came to his rescue. Stoutly declaring that they would stick together and that he would personally see that Steinmetz did not become destitute, Asmussen succeeded in having him admitted to the country which was to become for him the land of friends, fame, and fortune.

FROM TWELVE-DOLLAR-A-WEEK DRAFTSMAN TO THE WIZARD OF SCHENECTADY

His first application for work ended in failure. Armed with letters of introduction which he had brought from Zurich, he sought out the engineer of the Edison machine works, only to be told that "there was a regular epidemic of electricians coming to America."[2] The engineer looked only cursorily at a letter of introduction, couldn't understand his German or his copybook English, and so waved him out of the office.

Yet good fortune soon came in the form of Rudolf Eichmeyer, a manufacturer of hat machinery and electrical devices. It was only after hurdling the obstacle of an office clerk, who observed Steinmetz's poor clothes and his deformity and became suspicious of him, that Steinmetz gained an audience with Mr. Eichmeyer. This man's first words, "Sprechen Sie Deutsch, bitte," were the

---

[2] Hammond, J. W., *op. cit.,* p. 131.

finest Steinmetz had heard since arriving in America. It was not long before he and Eichmeyer were involved in a long conversation on technical problems. Furthermore, Eichmeyer suggested that he return at the end of a week. Great was Steinmetz's delight, upon returning, to be offered a position as a draftsman at a wage of twelve dollars per week. Now having secured a position, he speedily appeared before a naturalization court and took out his first papers. He wanted to be a worth-while citizen of the country to which he had come.

But the draftsman did not long remain such. The active mind of the new employee did not find enough occupation in merely making drawings for hat-making machinery. All over the country men were trying blindly to construct electrical generators and transformers. Steinmetz realized the need of theoretical knowledge in the process. Mathematics must be called to aid if electrical equipment was to be made dependable. To that task the humble draftsman set himself. He spent long hours after work experimenting with all sorts of metal and all kinds of current. Ferociously he dug into the problem, forgetting to sleep.

The reward for all this eventually came. On the evening of January 19, 1892, he read before the American Institute of Electrical Engineers a paper on "The Law of Hysteresis" which set forth discoveries eliminating a great deal of uncertainty in the designing of electrical equipment. Many an electrical engineer has offered a silent prayer of gratitude for the labors of this twenty-eight-year-old immigrant lad.

Still greater things were in store. The newly formed General Electric Company acquired the rights of the Eichmeyer company, consolidating the business with its own which was at that time located in Lynn, Massachusetts. Among the clauses of the sale contract was one which required Eichmeyer to persuade Steinmetz to go with General Electric. While he did not like the idea of going to Lynn, the fact that Eichmeyer had told him to go was enough. He would never have thought of deserting the ship merely because it had a new owner. He was as much a part of the company as any of the furniture which they had bought—and about as likely to stay behind. So he departed dutifully for Lynn, soon to find himself ensconced in a non-too-pleasant boarding-house.

An incident concerning his first days in Lynn is illustrative of the self-abnegation and self-forgetfulnes of the man. For the first few weeks that he was with the company in Lynn, through an oversight, he received no salary. Due to a clerical error his name had not been entered upon the payroll; but rather than complain, he used up his own meager savings, and was worrying himself sick lest his frail body might suddenly snap under the strain. But for the sudden intervention of a friend, serious consequences might have resulted.[3]

A few years later, when the General Electric Company moved to Schenectady, Steinmetz went along. For several years he had been giving serious attention to a study of alternating current. Although some leaders in the industry realized that progress was impossible with direct current, there were a great many who sought to block the introduction of alternating current. But the General Electric Company was instrumental in overcoming this opposition. They taught the public that alternating current was just as safe to use as direct and that, furthermore, it was vastly cheaper and more convenient. Back of this victory by the General Electric Company stood the prodigious calculations of the tiny hunchback whom they had acquired from the Eichmeyer company. Anyone who visits a large library today can see the books which record the result of all this calculating and experimenting. *Steinmetz on Alternating Current* is still a source book in the field. Although now one of the classics of electricity, four years elapsed from the time it was compiled until it was published.

If he had done nothing else, that work was enough to have brought him fame. But he did much more. He remained with the General Electric Company some thirty years, during which time he took out more than two hundred patents for electrical inventions. While it has been truly pointed out that these were not

[3] Leonard, Jonathan Norton, *Loki, the Life of Charles Proetus Steinmetz,* Doubleday, Doran & Co., New York, 1929, pp. 127-129.

sensational, they were all sound and serviceable. The devices and methods which he developed were largely concerned with those parts of electricity which are hidden from the general public. This made them hard to popularize. Yet it is quite fair to say that the great General Electric Corporation of today owes much to the labors of the little deformed "wizard of Schenectady."

THE REAL STEINMETZ

When on the morning of October 26, 1923, Steinmetz passed quietly away as the result of a heart attack suffered some days before upon his return from a trip to the Pacific coast for a convention of the American Institute of Electrical Engineers, the general public mourned his loss. But to most of them the man they mourned was a mystical figure built up by the publicity men. Most people thought of him as a wonder-worker standing in his laboratory surrounded by tremendous machines, manipulating powerful forces bottled in fragile glass containers, forces which, at word from the wizard, would leap forth destructively. But how few knew him as the man who served for more than a decade on the Board of Education of the city of Schenectady, or again for almost a decade as president of the Schenectady Common Council. How many knew of the hours of time he devoted to the duties of the president of the National Association of Corporation Schools, an organization which sought to correlate the educational opportunities of all those engaged in industrial work, so that inefficiency might be lessened and production speeded up. It was believed that this would help to raise the standard of living for workers.[4]

Few people thought of him as a college professor, though he was. In fact, teaching was one of his chief joys. In the year 1902 he accepted the professorship of electrical engineering at Union College in Schenectady, and through his efforts during the decade in which he labored there, the college came to be considered one of the best for the study of electrical engineering. He had the two qualities which make a great teacher—patience and the ability to

---

[4] Beard, Annie E. S., *Our Foreign-Born Citizens*, New York, Thos. Y. Crowell Co., 1922, pp. 257-258.

make things clear to another. His service for Union College illustrates something of the character of the man, for in all his years on the faculty he never received any remuneration.

THE GREATNESS OF THE MAN

There is good reason to believe that Steinmetz was never fully appreciated by the men for whom he labored, just as he was misunderstood by the public in general. Small of body and massive of head, he was equally massive of heart. To those about him he no doubt appeared as something of an oddity. Many of them were not of the caliber to understand and to appreciate him. He lived his quiet life in the midst of practical organizers, men of the world, those who knew "how to cash in." This he never did. Steinmetz felt every moment what his work meant in terms of ordinary human beings. He was of a different stripe from those about him; he was one of those "who do not cash in." That is why the little humpbacked figure of Charles P. Steinmetz stands out vividly from all the rest.[5] Not only the General Electric Company, but the world at large, could read with a sense of loss the two lines printed in the annual report to stockholders which the company issued a few months after his death. Could it have been put into figures it would have appeared on the debit side of the ledger and would have weighed heavily against the profits reported. This was the simple entry, but how much the words conveyed!

Dr. Charles P. Steinmetz died on October 26, 1923, after thirty years of devoted service to your company.[6]

For Discussion

1. When Dr. Steinmetz died it was discovered that he did not leave much of a fortune, yet had he cared to, he could have capitalized on his inventions so as to have become a rich man. What do you think of his attitude in this matter?

2. Some have said that when being persecuted as a Socialist, Stein-

---

[5] Passos, J. Dos, "Edison and Steinmetz: medicine men," *New Republic,* Dec. 18, 1929, p. 104.

[6] Leonard, J. N., *op. cit.,* p. 291.

metz exhibited cowardice when he departed from Germany to go to Austria. Would you so class him? Why?

3. Some men are born crooked of body and become also "warped of soul." What is there in the story of Dr. Steinmetz to indicate that this was not true in his case?

4. The religious creed of Dr. Steinmetz might be summed up by the phrase, "No human being should engage in an unsocial act." What do you think of the adequacy or inadequacy of this statement as the basis of a religious faith?

5. It is the contention of J. Dos Passos that the European view of America is that America does not produce first-rate men—men 'who do not cash in.' In your opinion, are the Europeans right?

6. The little-boy spirit in Dr. Steinmetz never died. He was always a lover of children and of children's games. Was this to his credit or discredit?

For Further Reading

Hammond, John W., *Charles Proteus Steinmetz*, D. Appleton-Century, New York, 1935.

Leonard, Jonathan N., *Loki, the Life of Charles Proteus Steinmetz,* Doubleday, Doran & Co., New York, 1929.

Beard, Annie E. S., *Our Foreign-Born Citizens,* Thomas Y. Crowell Co., New York, 1922. Chapter on "A Many-sided Genius."

Hammond, John W., "Charles P. Steinmetz, the Story of His Life and Works," *Mentor,* May, 1925, pp. 1-22.

Kennelly, A. E., "Charles P. Steinmetz, an Obituary," *Proceedings of the American Academy of Arts and Sciences,* January, 1925, pp. 657-660.

Leonard, Jonathan N.: "Steinmetz, Jove of Science," *World's Work,* Jan.-March, 1929, Vol. 58, pp. 32-41, 58-65, 120-138.

Moyer, L. W., *Lightning in the Laboratory;* a radio drama based on the life of Charles P. Steinmetz, *Scholastic,* December 10, 1938, pp. 17-19.

Passos, J. Dos, "Edison and Steinmetz: medicine men," *New Republic,* December 18, 1929, pp. 103-104.

Fannie Hurst

Celebrated Author

by

MYRTLE LECKY GRIMSHAW

I am passionately anxious to awake in people in general a sensitiveness to small people.

—FANNIE HURST

AN AUTHOR GROWS UP

ONCE THERE LIVED IN ST. LOUIS a lonely little girl, who spent many of her hours at the windows, peering out between the lace curtains at a world in which she took little part. There were neither brothers nor sisters nor even cousins with whom she could play. She lived in a world of adults, carefully secluded from outside contacts. Little wonder it is that young Fannie grew restive in this grown-up atmosphere and created imaginary young playmates with whom to spend her days.

In New York City today there lives a woman who is concerned with events and vividly portrays the people whom she still sees through her "mind's eye." But today we all know these companions of Fannie Hurst. We have read about them in her short stories and novels. We have seen them in the movies. Miss Hurst the woman is often a contrast to Fannie the child. No longer is her life secluded. The world is her life. There are few more vivid personalities or better-known women in contemporary America.

As one looks at Fannie Hurst, the writer, he sees that there were first fancies and people "in her head"; then later fancies and living people put down on paper for all to see. Once there was this little girl who made up playmates. Surely, the next step was to put them on paper. Or so Fannie believed; but it proved a long step, indeed.

A glance at her life will better reveal how Fannie, the daydreaming child, became Fannie Hurst, the celebrated writer.

EARLY LIFE OF FANNIE HURST

Fannie Hurst was born October 19, 1889, in the homestead of her grandparents in Hamilton, Ohio. Very soon after birth she was taken to their home in St. Louis by her Jewish parents, Samuel Hurst and Rose Koppel Hurst.

As she grew older she rebelled against a too pleasant and easy existence. Her boundless energy and unlimited interests did not fit her to live a comfortable, uneventful life. In high school she did her work brilliantly and with ease so she still had time to put her fancies on paper. At the age of fourteen she had already received a number of literary rejections.

During her years at Washington University she was equally recognized in the classroom, in athletics, and in extracurricular activities. In the midst of this busy college career she found time for prolific writing. She herself was unable to keep account of all her attempts, but no less than twenty-one stories were rejected by one magazine alone during this time.

After receiving her A.B. degree she tried teaching for a short time but her efforts were not successful. Then, still under twenty-one, she decided to storm the enemy in his own territory, and so moved to New York to wage her war against unappreciative editors. But her warfare was waged chiefly with the office boys, for she never once gained admittance to an editor's inner office during those early New York years.

DAYS OF A LEARNING AUTHOR

Her move to New York in itself was a miracle. Back in 1910, young girls of Fannie Hurst's position and family did not leave the parental fireside to gain experience in the big city—that is, not many did. However, Fannie was not the conventional young lady of her day and on the pretext of studying at Columbia she made her escape. Once there she took a three-hour course in Anglo-Saxon but between class sessions she wrote, rewrote and tried to peddle her manuscripts. For twenty-six months she worked

long hours every day on the stories she could not sell. She stayed
on in a city where she knew no one—in the face of parental opposition manifested in a dwindling allowance from home.

In addition to her writing she deliberately courted experience
to gain background for her stories. Her first New Year's Eve in
New York was spent along the Bowery. She had supper in a hobo
shelter and walked the streets until dawn.[1]

She was not satisfied with mere ramblings in the poorer streets
of the East Side and she determined to share the experiences of
these people. For a week she was a salesgirl in a department store.
It is said that among other things she worked as a waitress at
Childs' and even as a laborer in a sweat-shop. For a time she had
a negligible role on the stage. She lived over an Armenian tobac-
conist's shop in one of the foreign sections of the city. She went
steerage to Europe. What any other person could endure, so could
Fannie Hurst. It is true that she did not endure these hardships for
long periods of time, but it was sufficient for her to gain a sympathy
for and a perspective of the "little people" of the world. In later
days of acclaim she never forgot these early lessons.

Success did come eventually when one day she met an editor!
Robert Davis of Munsey's at last had recognized the merit of some
of her stories. Others followed his example. Immediately her
stories and even her opinions on this and that topic began to carry
weight with the previously inaccessible editorial staffs.

Soon after the publication of her first book, Miss Hurst married
Jacques S. Danielson, pianist and composer. The marriage has
been a happy one. Undoubtedly this marriage, as well as her
native Jewish love of music, has to some extent influenced her
writing, for both in theme and in the manner of presentation
music is dominant in many of her best stories.

The titles of some of her books indicate her deep interest in
music: *Every Soul Hath Its Song, Gaslight Sonatas, Humoresque,
Song of Life,* and *Anitra's Dance.*

In the novel *Anitra's Dance* the action centers around the musician, Rudolph Bruno, whose whole life is contained in his desire

---

[1] Salpeter, Harry, "Fannie Hurst—Sob-Sister of American Fiction," *Bookman,* August, 1931, p. 615.

to successfully complete his Span of Life Symphony. In the first chapter a part of his symphonic score is given to show the impasse of the unfinished theme. The book closes with a presentation of the finished score.

Days of a Successful Author

It was in 1914, with the publication of her first book, *Just Around The Corner,* a collection of short stories, that Miss Hurst became an acclaimed writer. Having won recognition, she retained it because of the merit of her later books. She was able to write these books because she did not depend on her definite and unusual talent, but because she was willing to use it in a ten-hour-day, six-day-week working schedule. Fortunately, Miss Hurst has always had superb health and unlimited vitality so that she still has had time and energy to live near to life. She finds time not only for intimate friendships and the lighter aspects of life, but for the world and many of its problems. The cause of the factory worker and of the miner she has made her own. She is a frequent first-nighter at the theater; she is likewise a frequent speaker in behalf of the laboring man.

In fact, Miss Hurst has been in the fore of so many good causes that critics have accused her of seeking publicity. This is often the fate of the public-spirited citizen. Miss Hurst never has been one of that too discriminating group who look so long they never leap even though a vital issue be at stake.

She is a clever woman, well-dressed and outstandingly smart in her New York environment. She is a connoisseur of art and a skillful collector. Florentine art dominates her apartment with its cathedral-like study. At the same time she is a friend of many of the less privileged people, a woman who has an honest appreciation and a canny understanding of them.

What Her Books Are About

Her books gain rather than lose from these contacts with the world of people. As their interpreter she is a writer with a cause —the broad cause of portraying situations and people, particularly the underprivileged, as they actually are.

On the other hand, she is not at all reluctant to picture the so-called important people as they actually are. Mrs. Farley, one of the characters in the novel *Lummox,* is a case in point. Mrs. Farley was active in the work of the Human Welfare League and considered herself interested in humanity. Yet her cook, Bertha, slept in the attic on a bed that sagged like a hammock. In her room under the sloping roof there was no heat in winter, and in summer no fresh air ever penetrated it.

The novel *Five and Ten* is the story of the world's thirteenth richest man and his family—a family for the most part of conflicting make-ups. Here were a wife and children belonging to the big people financially. Yet in many ways they were too small in stature to surmount the handicap of great wealth.

These characterizations go beyond a mere photographic reproduction, though there is that too. The discerning reader catches subtle glimpses of the deeper meanings of life. He senses that elusive mystical element that all great arts try to fix for even a fleeting moment.

Fannie Hurst has written many diverse novels and short stories. It is unfair, as well as impossible, to consider them as one continuous work and attribute the same characteristics to all. Yet many of her writings do have certain aspects in common. Miss Hurst always reveals her interest in "just a life." She herself once said: "I am passionately anxious to awake in people in general a sensitiveness to small people." [2]

She dislikes situations where *things* have become more important than *people,* because all people have meaning for her. Among her short stories one finds sympathetic studies of Jewish life, of six-dollar-a-week girls at bargain counters, of chorus girls and manicurists, of freaks, and of poorly clad slum children.

The novel *Lummox* is Miss Hurst's outstanding contribution to English literature. Vernon Loggins[3] believes it to be the best novel of its kind in American literature. Grant Overton[4] says that the

[2] H. Salpeter, *op. cit.,* p. 613.
[3] *I Hear America,* Thomas Y. Crowell Co., New York, 1937. Chapter on "Mindful of the Millions."
[4] *Women Who Make Our Novels,* Dodd, Mead & Co., New York, 1928. Chapter on "Fannie Hurst."

heroine of *Lummox* belongs with the great creations of fiction.

Lummox grew out of her sympathetic interest in the inarticulate thousands of submerged people. Bertha, the Swedish maid dubbed Lummox, blundered through life, clumsy and stupid. She was slow-witted, but kind—so kind that she became an easy mark for her employers. She broke the strict law of conventional morality, but her whole life was lived in sacrificial love. *Lummox,* the saga of Bertha, the Scandinavian drudge, has been favorably compared with Dickens' *David Copperfield.*[5]

Back Street, Imitation of Life, Four Daughters are all novels which occupy positions of merit in the field of American letters, but perhaps the novel *A President Is Born* is most imposing from a structural point of view. This is the story of the boyhood and youth of David Schuyler, who later became president of the United States. The book is written as though at some future year in our history. Yet the reader has no sense of unreality in adapting himself to Miss Hurst's liberties with the element of time. The footnotes supposedly taken from family diaries and documents ring true. It is not an account of politics, but the story of a family and an American town. Many critics have rated this book as one of America's great novels.

What Her Books Are Like

Fannie Hurst, like so many Jews, has an emotional insight into the lives of men. In her novel *Great Laughter* there is the account of Lawrence Campbell, who possessed and expressed emotions to a degree surprising in a Scotchman. This fact he himself laughingly attributed to the one per cent of one per cent strain of Pole and Jew which had worked into his blood stream by the way of a remote Semitic ancestor. Miss Hurst traces the meanderings of this Semitic strain down through the generations that followed him.

There may be more truth in such a theory than the scoffing people of *Great Laughter* believed. Certainly this emotional response to life, this quickening of spirit and intellectual probing into the depths of causes and events, so typical of Fannie Hurst, is an outstanding Jewish characteristic. Perhaps Miss Hurst should be

---

[5] V. Loggins, *op. cit.*, p. 347.

grateful to her Semitic background for her own sensitivity of perception.

The criticism has often been made that not always is Fannie Hurst pleasant reading. The answer to this is, of course, that not always is life itself pleasant. Miss Hurst seeks a truthful presentation of life. In one-hundred-year-old Gregrannie of *Great Laughter* there rose an "immense dreary laughter at what men will sweat for." It is unfortunate that such awareness does not rise in mankind as a whole.

Critics have compared Miss Hurst to O. Henry, to Dickens, and to Edna Ferber, but always with reservations and involved explanations of the differences. There is an elusive quality that is a part of all her writings. Why not merely say: "This is Fannie Hurst!"

But suppose one is determined to ferret out the exact explanation of Miss Hurst's talent. Then there must be considered such characteristics as her lively sense of humor, her mingling of the mystical and the sensual, of honest realism and romanticism. Miss Hurst has a definite technical skill that is evidenced particularly in her characterizations. Bertha the Lummox, whose J's melted in her throat, and who looked "Swedishly" with her broad face and "pitched-tent cheek bones," is a character any writer might be proud to have created.

Miss Hurst has a delightful way of turning a phrase that fills her books with bits worthy of quotation. She speaks of "the disorder of the day," and there is, for instance, Louis who, when shocked with bad news, had "sensations of trays falling down the stairs of his mind."

The personality of Fannie Hurst permeates her stories. They are stamped by her own peculiar genius. The best way to understand her is to read her books.

Study Hour Project

Have someone who is competent to do so give a book review of one of Miss Hurst's novels. If this is not feasible, have someone read aloud one of her short stories such as "Sunday Afternoon" in the *Woman's Home Companion*, July, 1940.

Additional Discussion

1. Is it too far-fetched to feel there is a certain kinship between Miss Hurst and the Old Testament prophet, Amos, who thundered, "Ye have sold the righteous for silver, and the needy for a pair of shoes"?

2. Miss Hurst once said: "I try to live each day intensely, knowing it will never come again." [6] How has this attitude been indicated in her life and work?

3. Could a struggle against a too easy life be as real as a struggle against poverty?

4. Using the life of Miss Hurst as an example, give suggestions as to how one might become a successful author.

Suggestions for Further Reading

I. Books by Miss Hurst.
   Read any or all of her short story collections. These are found in most libraries. Her first book *Just Around The Corner* is one of the most colorful. Read any or all of her novels. You might start with *Lummox, A President Is Born, Great Laughter*. It should be kept in mind that these are all books for mature-minded people.

II. Books and articles about Miss Hurst.
   1. Loggins, Vernon, *I Hear America.* Thos. Y. Crowell Co., New York, 1937, Chapter on "Mindful of the Millions."
   2. Overton, Grant, *Women Who Make Our Novels.* Dodd, Mead & Co., New York, 1928. Chapter on "Fannie Hurst."
   3. Collins, Joseph, *Taking the Literary Pulse.* George H. Doran Co., New York, 1924. Chapter on "Gallantry and Women Writers."
   4. "Fannie Hurst," by herself. *Mentor,* April, 1928, pp. 50-51.
   5. Salpeter, Harry, "Fannie Hurst, Sob-Sister of American Fiction," *Bookman,* August 1931, pp. 612-15.

---

[6] "You Too Can Stay Young," *Independent Woman,* January, 1938, p. 10.

Paul Muni

Master Character Actor

by

MYRTLE LECKY GRIMSHAW

In life people don't act they react. Actors must do the same.

—PAUL MUNI

EARLY LIFE

BACK IN THE EARLY 1900's a group of street urchins playing on the sidewalks of the New York Bowery suddenly filled the air with startled cries as they scattered here and there to clear the sidewalk. There had abruptly appeared in their midst a doddering old man on roller skates. Rather, he should have been doddering. His white hair hung to his shoulders; his beard swayed in the breeze; his face was weazened. He looked sick and feeble, but his actions belied his appearance. He was quick and nimble, darting here and there in fancy turns on his roller skates. How were these youngsters to know that this was eleven-year-old Paul Muni in his theater make-up and costume, out for his exercise between his stage appearances at the old Yiddish Theater of the Bowery?[1]

But to go back eleven years in his history. He was born in Lemberg, Austria, September 22, 1895, and was given the name Muni. His parents Salli and Phillip Weisenfreund were Jewish actors who traveled throughout Europe to appear in the continental Ghetto theaters. Times were hard and money scarce in Jewish quarters and although Weisenfreunds were talented, it was a struggle for the family to save money to migrate to America. Nevertheless, when Muni was still a small boy they came to the new land.

---

[1] Eustis, Morton, "Paul Muni—A Profile and Self-Portrait," *Theatre Arts,* March, 1940, p. 196 (Could this story be apocryphal?)

In New York they became a part of the Yiddish Theater group in the Bowery. It was while this company was on tour in Cleveland, presenting the play *Two Corpses at the Breakfast Table,* that the character actor taking the part of a feeble old banker became suddenly ill just before time for curtain call. There was no one else available so eleven-year-old Muni was pressed into service. He did so well that he continued in the part even when the company returned to New York. It is difficult to imagine an eleven-year-old boy possessing the skill and understanding necessary for such an undertaking, but neither is it easy to comprehend the ability of the grown Paul Muni, who creates characterizations of such utterly different personalities.

When the run of *Two Corpses* was over, Muni went back to his studies, for the father did not want any of his three sons to become an actor. He hoped that the three small Weisenfreunds would become great musicians. The combined income of the father and mother was only about thirty-five dollars a week. Sometimes a third of this went to pay for violin lessons for the three boys. The parents insisted upon a three-hour daily practice schedule. Often the family went without essential things in order to attend concerts.

At the age of thirteen, Muni took matters into his own hands. He decided to become an actor and refused to practice on his violin. This revolt against parental authority in a Jewish home the type of the Weisenfreund's must have been near-tragedy to the father and mother. The father broke Muni's violin and refused to speak to him for a time—or so the story goes. But at last one day the father said to Muni: "Well, if you're going to be an actor, don't be a ham." [2]

There then began a rigid training under the tutelage of his father when Muni joined New York's Yiddish Art Theater. A little later the Weisenfreunds moved to Chicago where they ran their own theater. Here Muni appeared. After all, he did save the expense of hiring another actor at ten dollars a week. This little movie and vaudeville theater, located at Twelfth and Hal-

[2] Beatty, Jerome, "The Man Who Is Always Somebody Else," *American Magazine,* February, 1938, p. 87.

sted streets, charged ten cents admission and was very much a
family affair. Mother, father, and Muni were actors. Muni's two
brothers comprised the piano and violin orchestra.

ON HIS OWN

When Muni was but fifteen his father died, and his mother returned to the East. Muni stayed on in Chicago for a time. Then
from 1914 to 1917 he appeared with a traveling troupe in many
of the Midwestern states. From 1917 to 1918 he played at the
Girard Street Theater in Philadelphia. For the next seven years
he was a member of the stock company of the Yiddish Art Theater
in New York.

When he was twenty-six years old he married Bella Finkle, also
renowned on the Yiddish stage. In fact, the Finkle name was to
New York's Lower East Side what the name Barrymore was to
Broadway.[3]

Muni himself has said that one learns to act by acting. These
were the years of his apprenticeship. He had parts in countless
plays and created a different type of characterization in each. He
received the rigorous training which is the advantage of stock companies. Whatever he did, he did with sincerity. He never took
advantage of any of the cheap little short cuts, the mannerisms and
attitudes sometimes used to draw attention to one actor at the expense of another. Each performance was an honest one.

BROADWAY AND HOLLYWOOD

It is not often that Broadway producers are interested in actors
of the Yiddish group. But when the Broadway play *We Americans*
was being cast, a theatrical scout brought in Muni's name for the
part of the old Jewish man. When Muni came for an interview
the producer was unsympathetic because of his youthful appearance. It is said that then and there, in the producer's presence,
Muni made up for the part and went into the characterization.[4]
He secured the role and did it so well the producers forgot about
his youth and thought of him in terms of his characterization. The

---

[3] Beatty, J., *op. cit.,* p. 88.
[4] Eustis, M., *op. cit.,* p. 196.

following year he had similar difficulty in securing the part of the young man in the prison drama *Four Walls.* This time he was so successful that rumors of his ability reached Hollywood.

The film *The Valiant,* in which he played the lead in a straightforward manner, was one of Hollywood's first talkies. His next film *Seven Faces* was not a success from the box-office point of view.

Around this time he did a couple of plays on Broadway in which his own portrayals were memorable, although the plays themselves were not particularly successful.

The turning point of his career came with his Hollywood opportunity to do *Scarface.* When this chance came, he was undecided whether or not to take it. It was his wife Bella who made the decision. She accepted the Hollywood offer and then wrote the absent Muni: "I have sold you down the river. Come home. We're leaving for Hollywood tomorrow."[5] His magnificent characterization gained Hollywood's approval, but for long months the finished film lay "canned" because of the Hays office trepidation regarding gangster pictures.

His return to New York to take the part of the grim young attorney in Elmer Rice's *Counsellor at Law* was welcomed on Broadway. His amazingly good performance would have secured him a permanent place on Broadway, but at last *Scarface* was revised and released. Overnight he became known and acclaimed by the thousands of movie-goers throughout the United States. He decided to throw in his lot with Hollywood. Muni Weisenfreund was a difficult name for movie-goers to remember and so he had adopted Paul Muni as a substitute at the beginning of his Hollywood career.

HIS CHARACTERIZATIONS

After his successful *Scarface,* he made the picture *I Am a Fugitive from the Chain Gang.* Because of his ability he escaped "typing," which has been the handicap of so many Hollywood character actors.

Without doubt Paul Muni has played more diversified roles

---

[5] Beatty, J., *op. cit.,* pp. 89-90.

than anyone in Hollywood. His characterizations have ranged from "machine-gun artist to captain of industry; from fugitive from justice to news reporter; from Mexican tough boy to a coal miner; from French man of science to a Chinese peasant."[6]

He was the industrial magnate in *The World Changes,* a news reporter in *Hi, Nellie,* a Mexican half-breed in *Bordertown,* a Polish miner in *Black Fury.* For his part in *The Story of Louis Pasteur,* he received in March, 1937, Hollywood's "Oscar," the actor's award of the Motion Picture Academy of Arts and Sciences. This film helped to prove to Hollywood that a biographical picture of merit, well done, can have box-office appeal. For thousands of people to whom he had been but a name, Paul Muni made Louis Pasteur a living personality.

His role as Wang in *The Good Earth* was a memorable one. His characterizations in *Zola, Juarez, We Are Not Alone,* were likewise well done. Most critics liked his work in *Zola* better than that in the two later plays. In his entire career, Paul Muni has never done a slipshod, an inartistic, or an unrealistic piece of work.

In discussing Muni's methods of work, his characterization of Emile Zola will serve as a ready example. One critic wrote that the *Zola* film achieved a validity of its own, for Muni had caught the spirit of the crusading French novelist.[7]

One recalls the history of *Zola,* villain and hero; how he had risen from the slums until he had become wealthy, fat, and indifferent to the affairs of mankind. His one consuming interest was to be elected to the French Academy. Then at last, as he became aware of the Dreyfus affair, the fires of his social conscience were rekindled. Captain Alfred Dreyfus had been falsely accused of treason, and after a farcical trial had been sent to Devil's Island. When Zola received the letter electing him to a place in the French Academy, he weighed it against the letters of appeal from Madame Dreyfus, knowing he must choose between them. There were a few moments of agonizing indecision. Then one recalls how Zola began writing "I Accuse!" If Muni had been less successful, such rec-

---

[6] "Muni, Paul—Master Character Actor," *Scholastic,* September 18, 1937, p. 39.

[7] *Newsweek,* August 14, 1937, p. 19.

ollections would be expressed in terms of Paul Muni as Zola. Rather, it is Zola alone who is remembered, for the movie-goer was not conscious of the man Muni. So it is with all his plays. At least so far as his audience is concerned, Paul Muni *is* the man whom he portrays.

Everyone realizes that Muni's characterizations are successful. Why they are and how he accomplishes his artistry is another matter. Muni himself does not help much in such a study. He is not good at self-analysis—at least not for public consumption. When questioned regarding his methods Muni once said: "To evaluate the *abc's* of acting for the public is a little like undressing in public."[8]

Articles have been written explaining how Muni prepares for a part. Statements have come from Hollywood publicizing his methods. But the testimony of Muni has not always agreed with these. One report described Muni's method of experimenting with gestures to acquire ways of walking, talking and thinking like his subject, and told of his deliberately taking on certain gestures and habits. But Muni himself once said: "I try to grasp the mind of the character I'm playing. I think his thoughts and unconsciously they motivate my hands, my voice, my face, my body. You cannot become a good actor if you merely imitate—if you are thinking, 'Now I'll lift a hand, now I'll shrug my shoulders, now I'll get my face closer to the camera.' "[9]

In every interview Muni emphasizes the idea that acting is a mental process, that the body responds as the mind dictates.

It is doubtless true that Muni does spend hours of research before attempting a characterization. Perhaps he practices long speeches into a dictaphone as has been suggested. However, all his research is done so that his mind may grasp the intellectual and emotional reactions of the subject and in order that his thoughts may be the same as his subject's. He avoids all that would make him self-conscious. "In life people don't act," says Muni, "they react. Actors must do the same."[10]

---

[8] Eustis, M., *op. cit.*, p. 194.
[9] Beatty, J., *op. cit.*, p. 90.
[10] Eustis, M., *op. cit.*, p. 202.

When Muni has a new part to play, he first looks for lines of kinship between his own personality and that of the one he is to portray. He believes that every part he plays opens up reservoirs of feeling within himself—feelings which may be inactive and well hidden, but which are nevertheless present. These feelings are so stimulated by his intellectual understanding of the character that Muni naturally reacts as would the portrayed character in the same situations. When he portrays Pasteur, or Zola, or the English doctor in *We Are Not Alone,* he is still Paul Muni—but Paul Muni reacting exactly as the character he is portraying reacted to life and its various situations. No amount of analysis can exactly explain Paul Muni's art nor make clear just how he creates these living personalities. After all, he has never read a book on acting and does not know just how he does it.

REASONS FOR HIS SUCCESS

First of all, Paul Muni has made an outstanding contribution to the world because he is one of those fortunate individuals who are given ten talents rather than one. Other persons, however, have been given ten talents which they have buried. There are more factors than that of talent contributing to his success.

For one thing he has been willing to work hard. Acting is a serious job with him; while a play is in process nothing is allowed to interfere with his work. Memorization is not easy for him. Learning lines demands long and earnest concentration on his part. As Zola, his speech to the jury ran six and one-half minutes. He spent hours and days on that one speech alone. Concerning it he said: "I had to learn the speech so well that when I was addressing the jury I would never at any time realize that I was an actor delivering the lines. I must be Zola, fighting for justice for Captain Dreyfus who was suffering on Devil's Island." [11]

From Hollywood came the rumor that when he was off the set he lived as a recluse, still feeling and enacting his film characterization. This ridiculous legend arose, no doubt, because he is a serious worker who wastes little time in Hollywood's bright spots.

[11] Beatty, J., *op. cit.,* p. 86.

For another thing, he has been willing to adapt himself to changing situations. He was first trained in the classical traditions of the Yiddish stage and deliberately transplanted his life into the American theater. Still another change came when he left Broadway for Hollywood.[12] Instead of being dismayed by the change of technique in Hollywood, he profited by certain of its advantages. Accustoming himself to the lack of rehearsals and consecutive acting, he determined to learn his characterizations and his lines so well that he could always feel at ease in his part and be able to pick it up at any point in the play. He does not object to repeating his lines a dozen times so that the best results can be selected in the cutting room.

He has never resented criticism. Directors do not give him minute instructions, but let him work out his parts for himself. When they feel that he has somehow missed the mark they tell him and Muni tries again, always willing to seek perfection.

Muni feels that much of his success came to him by chance. He did, however, make one choice which partly determined his future —he married the right wife. Married over eighteen years to Paul Muni, Bella Muni has a large part in her husband's career. When they were married she was a skilled actress, and today she understands the Hollywood profession as do few others. She accompanies Muni to the set where she is an inconspicuous but a watchful critic. When Bella signals, the scene is done over. Paul Muni is easily discouraged. It is Bella who encourages when things go wrong. No wonder she guards his career, for she was enough interested in it to forsake her own.

Finally, Paul Muni could never have attained his present success had he not had ideals to which he has held throughout his years in Hollywood. When he first went to the film world, he came in contact with a group of people interested primarily in box-office returns. He could have cashed in on this interest had he wished. Instead, he demanded the right to choose his own plays. He did fewer plays, but those he did were worth while. He did not de-

---

[12] Clausen, Bernard C., "A Moment in the Conscience of Man," *The Christian Century,* December 1, 1937, p. 1484.

mand big parts, or a center-of-the-stage casting; but he did require
his role to be a worth-while characterization. That he finally rose
to a high salary was due to his great ability; not to any particular
desire for money. Certainly, Paul Muni is not an actor in order
to teach certain lessons to a dull world; nevertheless, the world
has had more beauty and truth because of Muni's career. We have
learned of social injustice in such plays as *I Am a Fugitive from the
Chain Gang* and *Black Fury*. We have seen true nobility in such
portraits as those of Pasteur and Zola. Even in these days of world
hatred and suspicions we can not entirely forget all tolerance, re-
membering *We Are Not Alone*. All art has truth for those who
are alert.

Muni has said he would never do a play which did not appeal
to him. When, for that reason, he had refused to make a picture
for several months, many people feared he had gone into retirement. Finally, he broke with his regular studio to do free-lancing.
Soon *Hudson's Bay Company* went into production, and more recently *Counterattack* was produced. In his portrayals of an adven-
turer and a Russian guerilla he did as careful and honest characterizations as he did of Pasteur and Zola. One remembers that Paul
Muni once said: "All I know about acting is that you must work
conscientiously. Don't understimate the intelligence of your audience—and don't cheat." [13]

Questions for Discussion

1. A certain philosopher once suggested that one should use half his
money for bread and half for hyacinths. Would the Weisenfreund family have agreed with such a philosophy?

2. What factors do you think contributed most toward Muni's
success?

3. What did you like best about each of the Muni movies you have
seen? Can you explain just why you liked certain pictures?

4. If you were a motion picture director, what books would you wish
dramatized as vehicles for Muni and what parts would you assign to him?

5. By the means of the drama, just what has Muni contributed to
the world other than entertainment? What contributions may he have
made by his refusal to act in certain plays.

[13] Beatty, J., *op. cit.*, p. 90.

Bibliography

Beatty, Jerome, "The Man Who is Always Somebody Else," *American Magazine*, February, 1938, pp. 42, 43 and 86-90.

Eustis, Morton, "Paul Muni—a Profile and Self-portrait," *Theatre Arts*, March, 1940, pp. 194-205.

Clausen, Bernard C., "A Moment in the Conscience of Man," *The Christian Century*, December 1, 1937, pp. 1484-85.

Biographical Sketch, *Newsweek*, August 14, 1937, p. 10.

"Muni, Paul—Master Character Actor," *Scholastic*, September 18, 1937, p. 39.

Yehudi Menuhin

Master of the Violin

by

GRACE CHAPIN AUTEN

Music resembles poetry; in each
Are nameless graces which no methods teach,
And which a master-hand alone can reach.

—ALEXANDE

TO ONE WHO HAS HEARD Yehudi Menuhin play
the experience stands out as one never to be forg
sit enraptured under the spell of his marvelous n
event of a lifetime. He was fourteen or fifteen years o.
heard him give a recital in St. Louis, Missouri. He wa.
haired, handsome, self-possessed, quiet lad, with dignity o1
ner, so thoroughly devoted to his art that he seemed almost i1
ferent to the tremendous ovation he received. The difficult mu.
sang from his bow with delicate shades of meaning, fluent, in¢.
pressibly free, exquisitely beautiful as only music can be unde
the interpretation of a great master. One wondered which was
most extraordinary, Yehudi's perfection of technique, or his de·
icacy and intelligence of musical interpretation, or just the ¹
himself in genius, intellect, and height of achievement. His ·
made his performance the more remarkable of course, f
eyes closed one would have supposed the musician ·
mature years. There was nothing about him of the ch
clamoring for attention. He has always felt that the ₁
is of far more consequence than any personal acclaim. :

Yehudi Menuhin is now a young man in the twenties
the world over as one of the greatest of living violin
certainly one of the most popular in America today. He

achieved more musical triumphs than many musicians in a lifetime. He has been called the greatest musical attraction in the world. But he remains unspoiled, modest, an earnest student, intellectually broad, quiet in his tastes, maintaining his high ideals, both in his art and in his character, working hard, living much in the open, with many natural interests, singularly free from greed of gain, ʹd shouldered and vigorous, cultured, friendly, devoted to ʹ nd family.

Martha and Moshe Menuhin, parents of this genius in music, e teachers living on a meager budget in New York City when he was born, April 22, 1917. His mother says they had no ʹ for this baby except that they might have means to feed him, and that he might be happy. His father was called ʹn in San Francisco and it was there that Yehudi, when ʹnths old, was taken to a symphony orchestra concert, there ʹ money to pay some one to care for him at home. His ʹ miled to see the baby's absorbed attention. At the age of ʹ was given a toy violin. When he discovered no true music ʹ threw it on the floor in a rage and stamped on it. His ʹ, writing of the incident, says that his parents then knew ʹ something exceedingly sensitive in the child had been out-ʹged. They could not afford a real violin, but Yehudi's grand-mother supplied one. His mother warned him not to make scratchy sounds on it. He never did, she says. When four he began studying with San Francisco artists, Sigmund Anker, then Louis Persinger. At five he played his first public concert for the Pacific Musical Society. When six he played Mendelssohn's great concerto in San Francisco. He was eight years old when he played his ʹ real professional concert with admissions charged. He played ʹimes to vast audiences during his childhood, but his parents ʹimited the number of his concert appearances and firmly ʹ exploit his genius, always insisting on long months of ʹ from public responsibilities. At ten his playing with the ʹ Symphony Orchestra in Carnegie Hall created a tremen-ʹ tion. Ever since, he has maintained and steadily in-ʹs reputation as an artist all over America, in England, ʹnd around the world.

He was still a boy when he went abroad with his parents and his two talented sisters for further study. The famous violinist and teacher, Georges Enesco, had given a concert in Paris one evening, and he was surprised to have a boy join the admiring circle congratulating him after the program. The boy said he wanted to see him. Enesco was impressed by the boy's manner and made an appointment for the next day. "I want to study with you," Yehudi announced quietly. Enesco asked him to play. From the first moment of Enesco's astonished listening, he welcomed Yehudi as his pupil and as his friend. Georges Enesco has no doubt been the greatest single influence in musical study that Yehudi has had. He had the privilege also of studying with Adolph Busch, the great Swiss violinist.

Yehudi has always given untiring effort and unceasing study in his own hours of practice, usually four hours a day, except Saturday and Sunday. Besides his education in music, he had tutors from time to time in other subjects; but his father and mother have been his chief teachers. His mother is a remarkable linguist, speaking some nine languages. She gave her three children proficiency in five or six languages. In 1938, Yehudi and his sisters could speak fluently English, French, German, Italian, Hebrew. Yehudi was learning Russian also.

Marutha Menuhin made education interesting. They had a blackboard in the kitchen, and while cooking dinner the mother talked, or they read a book in the original language in which it was written. Yehudi enjoys reading Tolstoi's books in Russian. Sometimes lessons were learned while sunning after a glorious swim in their own pool on the ranch in the hills of California, or while strolling in the moonlight with their mother. Yehudi's father was his teacher when they were on tour. He gave Yehudi problems in mathematics and science, and together they read books of history and literature. By clipping interesting items from many newspapers and later discussing these with his son, Moshe Menuhin developed Yehudi's unusual intelligence around a broad range of interests. Among subjects studied were geography, the customs and manners of other lands, history of art, history of music, physics, economics, and literature of several languages. Neither Yehudi nor his sisters attended school but fortunately their home environment, together with their opportunities for study and travel have given them each an enviable education. When asked how she accounted for Yehudi's genius, his mother replied that the children, Yehudi, Hepzibah and Yaltah, were merely living out the family tradition. On both sides, their ancestors have been linguists, musicians or lovers of music, physicians, teachers, home-loving idealists. Indeed, Yehudi's mother wished he might have been a physician, able to live more or less out of the public eye, pursuing his vocation in one place, instead of traveling all over the world. She used to think with dismay of all the practicing necessary in a musician's life.

Yehudi's maternal grandmother was an Italian lady; her husband, of Tartar descent, was born in the Crimea, a dreamer yet strangely wise. Yehudi's father was born in Russia, of Jewish descent, and brought up in Palestine, being educated at Jaffa. Both Moshe and Marutha must be of unusual intelligence, and wizards of skill in child-training and development. The truth is, they are also singularly free from false ambitions.

The Menuhins have consistently declined to be controlled by the tempo of modern life. They have been untempted by the easy possibility of making a huge fortune out of their son's fame. They have been unharmed by the world's plaudits or allurements. They hoped Yehudi's sister Hepzibah, of great talent as a pianist, would not have a musical career, feeling sure that her true happiness would be in home life. For long vacations, refusing all demands for concerts, they took their children to an ideal summer home in France, near Versailles, and let them enjoy the freedom of woods, water and fields; or to their beloved home in the Santa Cruz Mountains of California, where swimming, hiking, motoring, bicycling, badminton, tennis, practicing, were combined with the companionship of friends from all over the world. Best of all, always, has been the comradeship which characterized the Menuhin family among themselves.

Yehudi at fifteen allowed the publication in the *Etude* of an account of his own methods of study. The interview was secured by Rose Heylbut, and is entitled "How I Live and Work." (*Etude,*

Dec. 1932.) He does not think his methods necessarily the best, but for him they have proved of worth. He is accustomed to look over a piece of music, studying it thoroughly for problems of technique and for grasp of musical meaning. He always does this careful work on a selection before playing it at all. When he begins actual practice, he works out the technical points before playing with the full emotional meaning. He says that he always knows *inside* what he means to do with it when he finishes his practice of it. Frequently he would take a piece of music with him upon retiring and study it over, deciding on the composer's meaning and considering shades of expression. When studying with Enesco, Yehudi often played with little interruption from his teacher. However, when there seemed doubt as to a fine shade of meaning, Yehudi would try different ways of playing it until he felt satisfied he had discovered the composer's own intention. Enesco led his brilliant pupil to do a great deal of research work on the lives and compositions of the great masters, that by understanding their experiences, he might the better interpret their music. As he has developed, his artistic interpretation has grown and changed. He never feels that a composition of music once mastered is then to be set aside as finished; but rather that he may return to it to discover fresh meaning in it, or changed meaning, just as one reads Shakespeare, Browning or the Bible with deeper insight and appreciation as one grows older. Sometimes years of devoted study are needed for the maturing of a musical conception. In a working week Menuhin retires early, as he wants to bring serenity and freshness to the next morning's study. After complete relaxation over the week end, he returns on Monday morning with a "high sense of anticipation" to the problems yet unsolved. Each selection becomes to him not a succession of notes but a "single, coherent musical thought." As he says: "The search for one's own conception of the composer's meaning remains the purpose of all playing." One of Yehudi's goals has been familiarity with all the works of any composer that he is studying. He has been able to start on a concert tour with fifty great concertos in his repertoire. The absorbed intentness of Yehudi Menuhin's face as he plays suggests that he desires only to reproduce the full musical beauty of the original.

It was Enesco who advised keeping to but few concerts in the growing years; giving Yehudi plenty of rest, quiet, freedom. His mother even succeeded in securing a promise, which he fulfilled, of taking a two years' retirement after he returned from a brilliant world tour, during which he met one hundred and ten engagements in seventy-three cities and thirteen countries. The two years of retirement he spent quietly and delightfully at Los Gatos, their California home, with his parents and sisters. When he returned to the concert stage, his skill was enhanced and his vast fame more secure than ever before. He was immediately booked from September of 1937 to the summer of 1940 with concert offers and world tours. His sister Hepzibah, gifted pianist, sometimes appeared with him as his accompanist. They have made many broadcasts. They won the Candide prize for the best record made in France during one year. The 10,000 francs included as an additional honor were given by Yehudi and Hepzibah for assisting needy musicians in France.

Among Yehudi's friends are not only great artists, but noted men of letters and science. Toscanini, skeptical at first of Yehudi's power, had only to hear the boy play to hail him as a genius and become an enduring enthusiastic friend. The great scientist Einstein, after hearing the young violinist, exclaimed that Yehudi had once again proved to him that there is a God in heaven. Emil Ludwig, the historian; Bruno Walter, the famous orchestral director; Horowitz, the renowned pianist; and Piatigorsky, one of the most eminent of cellists, have been among the many famous guests at Los Gatos. They have loved to wander over the California hills in deep conversation. They enjoy the high thinking, the genuineness of life, the unaffected simplicity of purpose, the broad interests that characterize the Menuhin family.

Strangely enough, Yehudi and his two gifted sisters were all married within about two months of each other in 1938. Yehudi was married in London in May of that year to Nola Nicholas, vivacious young daughter of a rich Australian aspirin manufacturer.

Life of December 25, 1939, gave charming pictures of Yehudi, Nola, and their little baby daughter named Zamira. In Russian, Zamira means "Peace" and in Hebrew, "Nightingale." The photographs suggest that Yehudi is an affectionate and devoted father and husband. Yehudi and Nola now have a son, also, making home-joy complete.

It would be a long list if one were to record the full extent of Yehudi's musical triumphs. Two of them must always stand out in his memory—the phenomenal ovation he received from three thousand people at Carnegie Hall in New York City when he was ten years old, and that memorable outburst of acclaim from the vast audience at Leipzig on Nov. 14, 1931, which was the occasion of the one hundred fiftieth anniversary of the city's wonderful Gewandhaus. He had played Beethoven's concerto and Mendelssohn's concerto in the very city which is so full of associations of Mendelssohn's life work. Yehudi said this experience gave him a special feeling of awe and rapture. He received from the great composer's grandchildren their warm gratitude for his interpretation of their grandfather's beautiful concerto. After the concert, further honors followed at an elaborate banquet attended by over one hundred of Germany's greatest leaders in art, science, music and politics. The young violinist, fourteen years old at the time, was there declared a genius of the highest order, but his greatest happiness was not in the honors heaped upon himself but in having been chosen on that occasion to pay tribute to the Leipzig orchestra and in having the opportunity of bringing fresh laurels to the memory of Mendelssohn. Since then there have been innumerable concert triumphs.

Well has Menuhin followed the advice of his friend and teacher Georges Enesco, not to be disturbed by criticism or praise. Said he, "Do not look level, look above." Yehudi Menuhin's spirit has remained modest, reverent. His favorite composers are the classics, Bach, Beethoven, Brahms, Mozart. Through his opportunities for extensive research he has been able to present to the public many slightly known, or unknown, compositions, notably the so-called "lost concerto" of Schumann, beautiful in its pathos and power.

When Menuhin's wife called him at Fort Wayne, Indiana, where he was giving a concert, informing him that he had been rated class 1A in the draft he answered as follows: "If my country needs me, I shall be glad to serve. Of course I shall be happy to do my bit."

For Discussion

1. Contrast Yehudi Menuhin's younger years with that of certain other child-prodigies. How did his parents guard him from self-conceit, exploitation, and an unnatural childhood?

2. What has contributed most to make Menuhin a master among musical artists—natural genius, the opportunity to study with great teachers, or continued, devoted work?

3. What is your definition of *education?* Of true *culture?*

4. What is the "modern tempo" of life? Compare the modern tempo with the aims and ideals of the Menuhin family.

5. Account for the wide reach of Menuhin's friendships.

6. Discuss whether a true artist gives a recital to enhance his own fame, or to reveal the greatness of the composers whose music he plays.

7. Yehudi's mother states that she had no ambitions for her children except that they might be happy. Was she then not ambitious?

For Further Reading

Ewen, David, *Men and Women Who Make Music,* Thomas Y. Crowell Co., New York, 1939.

Wollstein, R. H., "The Goal Is Always Music," *Etude,* May, 1938.

Menuhin, Marutha, "Our Children and How They Grew." *Woman's Home Companion,* March, 1938.

————*Newsweek,* "Menuhin and Freedom," November, 1938.

Thompson, Oscar, (editor) *International Cyclopedia of Music and Musicians*— "Menuhin," Dodd, Mead Co., New York, 1926.

————*Life,* (pictures) Dec. 25, 1939.

Rose Heylbut, an article on Yehudi Menuhin, "How I Live and Work," *Etude,* December, 1932.

Lissfelt, J. Fred, "Yehudi Menuhin, An American Boy," *Scholastic,* Vol. 26, No. 1, February 2, 1935.

Grove, Sir George, "Menuhin, Yehudi," *Dictionary of Music and Musicians.* Supplementary volume edited by H. C. Colles, Macmillan, New York, 1940.

Dumesnil, Maurice, "Enesco Talks on Menuhin," *Etude,* February, 1937.

————"Tour's End," *Time,* March 30, 1936.

————"Menuhin, Yehudi," *Who's Who in America.*

Joseph Goldberger

Fighter of Pellagra

by

KARL R. STOLZ

Seeing how the world suffered and bled,
He said:
"My life shall bring
Help to that suffering."

—ANGELA MORGAN

D R. JOSEPH GOLDBERGER united in his personality and career the scientist, the humanitarian and the investigator. The story of his life is the story of a man who found joy, relaxation and repose in work that has brought hope and healing to multitudes of sick people. It is, in addition, the story of an immigrant boy who, through sheer ability, perseverance and common sense, became one of the most famous members of the medical profession in America.

As a contributor to medical science Dr. Goldberger devised no new surgical techniques and no vaccines or serums. He discovered no vitamins and created no new drug with startling potency. He detected no deadly germs. Although a man with a passion for research, he appears to have preferred personal and intimate contacts with the sick to the laboratory equipped with all the mechanical appliances the ingenuity of man has invented.

As a lad of seven, Joseph Goldberger was brought from Czechoslovakia to New York City by his parents in 1882. His father and mother were sturdy folk. The orthodox, bearded father was a grocer. Joseph attended the public schools of New York. He played on the swarming sidewalks. In due course of time, with the financial help of parents and brothers, he was graduated from the College of the City of New York. It was Joseph's ambition to be a mining engineer, but the hearing of a lecture delivered by a noted physician on a phase of medicine altered the plans of the lad. He resolved to be a doctor. He was awarded the M.D. degree by the Bellevue Hospital Medical College in 1895. After serving as a staff member of Bellevue Hospital he practiced medicine for two years in Wilkes-Barre, Pennsylvania.

Sustaining a competitive examination, Dr. Goldberger was appointed assistant surgeon in the United States Health Service, then known as the Marine Hospital Service. He was a commissioned officer in this branch of government service from 1899 until his untimely death in 1929. He crowded an amazing amount of productive work into these thirty years.

MEDICAL CONTRIBUTIONS

Dr. Goldberger is identified with the discovery of the cause, cure and prevention of a nutritional disease called pellagra. He contributed more than eighty-five articles to medical literature on a number of diseases such as black-tongue, influenza, hydrophobia, diphtheria, typhus fever, typhoid fever, yellow fever, measles, the straw itch, dengue fever and pellagra. Although his investigations and findings in various other areas of medicine are valuable, his discovery of the nature and treatment of pellagra is monumental. His fame rests on work that led to the conquest of a scourge that claimed uncounted victims each year.

What is pellagra? It is, as we now know, thanks to Dr. Goldberger and his associates, a disease caused by a diet deficiency. Its symptoms include eruption of the skin, weakness, nervousness, anxiety dreams and indigestion. In children the malady is marked by listlessness, fretfulness and loss of weight or underweight. The victims, unless the disease is checked, suffer severe and, in the end, fatal constitutional effects. Many pellagrins become insane.

The ravages of pellagra in Southern Europe and elsewhere attracted the attention and aroused the concern of economists and statesmen as well as physicians, long before Dr. Goldberger attacked the scourge. Medical literature takes cognizance of it as early as 1735. Many studies of the ailment were made and various theories of its source and treatment were advanced. Complex cures and remedies were recommended. Here and there an obscure family doctor declared that if a pellagrin were well fed the plague of the red rash and sore mouth would vanish. Such a statement then would be hotly denied by well-known physicians and scientists. Medical periodicals were replete with assertions that pellagra is a germ disease, or is induced by the bites of buffalo gnats, or by the eating of spoiled corn.

The origin and cure of pellagra remained quite uncertain until Dr. Goldberger made his investigations. It was he who scientifically disclosed the cause and prescribed the simple means for its cure and prevention.

Pellagra was first reported in the United States in 1907. The disease spread with such rapidity, especially in the South, that it became both a medical and economic problem in industrial and agricultural communities. In 1913 Dr. Goldberger, having shown outstanding ability in medical research, was commissioned by the surgeon-general of the Public Health Service at Washington, D. C., to undertake the study of the cause, cure and eradication of pellagra. With customary devotion, intelligence and efficiency Dr. Goldberger accepted the assignment. He did not have the disease brought to him in jars containing the bodily elements of the pellagrins. He invaded the haunts of pellagra and made personal studies of the sufferers.

For example, in 1914, a year when almost 1200 persons are recorded to have died of pellagra in Mississippi, he visited a Methodist orphanage at Jackson in that state. Seventy-nine of the inmates of the institution were definitely pellagrous. The diseased children displayed the characteristic symptoms of irritability, weakness, pain, nightmares and red rashes. Dr. Goldberger requested permission of the orphanage authorities to feed all the children fresh meat and plenty of milk, at the expense of the United States Public Health Service. Of course the permission was granted. The children were given generous portions of fresh protein foods. In a few months the saying, "once a pellagrin always a pellagrin," was challenged and eventually it was overthrown and retired. The children responded positively to a balanced diet.

For years the fallacy had persisted that pellagra is a communicable disease and originates in a harmful element in the patient's diet. Dr. Goldberger's findings disposed of both assumptions. His observations and investigations led to radically different conceptions of the nature of pellagra. He concluded that a hidden hunger is the cause of the disease.

He established the connection of a diet deficiency and pellagra. He placed it in the same general category with scurvy and beriberi. He patiently studied the bearing of environment, age and diet on the cases of pellagra with which he came into contact. His judiciously conducted experiments proved that recovery from or the prevention of pellagra can be accomplished by a balanced diet.

Such foods as eggs, milk, fresh lean meat and vegetables combat or preclude pellagra. Foods and vitamin complexes were explored with special reference to the conquest of this disease. Carrots and rutabagas, likewise cod liver oil and gelatine, it was determined, lack the elements which annihilate pellagra. On the other hand, in addition to the foods first mentioned, tomato juice, brewers' yeast and dried pig's liver were found to abound in the food values which prevent or exterminate pellagra. Dr. Goldberger and his associates continued their investigations for eleven years.

MAKING ASSURANCE DOUBLY SURE

According to an old saying, it is a poor rule that does not work both ways. Dr. Goldberger, Dr. Wheeler and others induced cases of pellagra by giving human beings unbalanced diets.

In 1914, a year already referred to as one when pellagra was especially prevalent, Dr. Goldberger made a unique request of Governor Brewer of Mississippi. The doctor explained that pellagra is a result of the lack of proper food. Dr. Goldberger petitioned the Governor for permission to give some of the convicts at the Rankin Prison Farm the same diet on which the pellagrins lived—and died. The doctor argued that if the convicts developed pellagra eating the same food the poor on the tenant farms and in the mill villages consumed, he could restore them to health by feeding them meat, milk and eggs.

Permission under certain conditions was granted. It was stipulated that the convict volunteers should subsist on the restricted diet for no more than six months, and that at the end of this period they were to be rewarded with their freedom. In other words, for living on corn pone, white bread, salt pork, grits, sweet potatoes, cane syrup and cabbage, and taking the consequences for a few months, they were to leave the prison as free men! Eleven convicts were placed on the ordinary diet of the poor in the South and kept under strict observation for half a year. Only a small amount of vegetables was given the subjects. No milk or meat or fruit was included in the diet.

Within five months, six of the eleven convicts, all of whom had been hale and hearty men, developed pellagra. None of these had previously displayed the pellagra symptoms. Rats restricted to the same deficient diet developed the same symptoms which pellagrous human beings exhibited.

At the expiration of the designated period, Dr. Goldberger begged the sick men to remain under his care for a few weeks longer in order that they might be cured through a balanced diet. The convicts were more eager to savor freedom than to continue as experimental subjects, even for their own good. The Governor had given them his word of honor and could not compel them to yield to the importunities of Dr. Goldberger. On November 1st they "passed from observation" as the record states.

Meanwhile, how were the convicts on the regular prison farm faring? They were dirty, pestered by cooties and bedbugs and living in crowded quarters, but not a single one of the hundreds had the rash, sore mouth, night terrors and nervousness symptomatic of pellagra. Their diet included fresh meat and milk. The two groups of convicts performed a perfect test.

Dr. Goldberger observed that in an asylum where the inmates became victims of pellagra none of the attendants, nurses and physicians were afflicted with the disease. The logical inference was that the exceptions resulted from a difference in diet. Supplied with generous allowances of fresh meat and vegetables and con-

siderable milk these persons, although in intimate contact with
pellagra patients, did not contract the disease. Evidently pellagra
was not a germ disease and was not communicable.

Pellagra is not transmissible from one person to another but
may be induced in an individual by a restricted diet. Studies made
by Dr. Goldberger and his collaborators revealed that the majority
of pellagra patients are children ranging from two to fifteen years
of age. During the first two years of life most children are fed with
milk. On the other hand, children from two to fifteen in underprivileged families in certain regions of our country have little
pocket money with which to buy food which supplements the unbalanced diet served at home. Furthermore, the incidence of pellagra is especially marked from April to July, the period of the
year when a balanced diet is either not provided or relished. There
is little or no pellagra among the wealthy or even the moderately
well-to-do.

Dr. Goldberger was a thorough man. In order to establish beyond a shadow of a doubt his contention that pellagra is not a
germ disease, he engaged in additional experiments. The blood,
excrement and the spinal fluid of pellagrins at the gate of death
had been injected into monkeys and baboons without disastrous
results. The sceptical argued that perhaps monkeys and baboons
are not subject to pellagra, and if a germ is responsible for the
dread disease, these animals may not be susceptible. Dr. Goldberger
resolved to use himself and his trusted helper, Dr. Wheeler, as
experimental subjects.

Blood from the arm of a woman desperately sick with pellagra
was drawn into a sterile syringe. Dr. Goldberger injected a portion
of the blood into the left shoulder of Dr. Wheeler. A part of an
ounce of the blood was injected by Dr. Wheeler into the shoulder
of Dr. Goldberger. The results were negative, neither of the men
developed pellagra.

Not yet persuaded that his contention of the origin and treatment of pellagra had been put to every conceivable test, Dr. Goldberger swallowed the intestinal discharge of a woman suffering
from a true case of the scourge. For good measure Dr. Goldberger
then swallowed a powder consisting of flour and the scaled-off skin

from the two other pellagrins. Although the doses upset Dr. Goldberger's stomach, no sign or symptom of pellagra appeared. Verily, Dr. Goldberger left no stone unturned in his investigations and experiments.

Dr. Goldberger engaged in his observations and experiments in such southern states as Tennessee, Arkansas, Mississippi and Louisiana. As already stated, he did not confine his investigations to pellagra. He studied the mode in which influenza, typhus and typhoid fever are transmitted. The inoculation of the monkey with diseases from the human being taught Dr. Goldberger many things which are medically useful. He showed that measles is transmissible only in its early stages. He ascertained the existence of a resemblance between black-tongue among dogs and pellagra among human beings.

A Lovable Man

While engaged in his researches Dr. Goldberger was thrice stricken with severe diseases. He was oblivious of personal danger, ignored his private interests, and took no thought of the comforts most men prize. His lovable disposition, his tolerance, his practical idealism, his unfailing sense of humor combined to endear him to all who knew him. He was more at home in the hovels of the poor than in the mansions of the prosperous and influential. Millions who will never even read of his accomplishments will be the beneficiaries of his labors of love. His life was not free from opposition and tribulation. He overcame scepticism and hostility, not by vituperation but by study, experimentation and publicity of his findings among readers of medical literature. Observable and provable data were his weapons against ignorance and disease.

He died at a comparatively early age, but his medical findings, adopted by the members of his profession, assure him an earthly immortality. Dr. Goldberger was a great physician because he was first, last and always a genuinely good man, a man on the heroic scale, a man who exemplified the grand dimensions of human nature.

For Discussion

1. Do the children of foreign-born parents prize advantages in America more than do the children of the American-born? State reasons for your conclusion.

2. Was the success of Dr. Goldberger as a medical investigator due to inborn qualities or environment?

3. Was the fact that he had to secure his education by the practice of self-denial on his part and on that of his parents and brothers a help or hindrance to his career?

4. Why, in your opinion, did he pursue researches at a comparatively modest salary when he might have engaged in a lucrative private practice?

5. What was the relation of his personal interest in people to his scientific accomplishments?

For Further Reading

Goldberger, Joseph, "Pellagra: Its Nature and Prevention," *Public Health Reports,* Vol. 33, pp. 481 ff.

————, "Experimental Pellagra in White Convicts," *Archives of Internal Medicine,* Vol. 25, pp. 451 ff.

————, "A Study of the Relation of Diet to Pellagra," *Public Health Reports,* Vol. 35. pp. 648 ff.

————, "A Study of the Treatment and Prevention of Pellagra," *Public Health Reports,* Vol. 39, pp. 87 ff.

Kagin, Solomon R., "Joseph Goldberger (1874-1929)," *Medical Record,* Vol. 146, pp. 473 ff.

————, "Jewish Contributions to Medicine in America," *Medical Life,* Vol. 40, pp. 435 ff.

Dearman, W. A., "Tribute to Dr. Joseph Goldberger," *New Orleans Medical and Surgical Journal,* Vol. 88, pp. 139 ff.

Records of the House of Representatives for 1929.

Carl Laemmle

Motion Picture Producer

by

KARL R. STOLZ

Man must pass from old to new,
From vain to real, from mistake to fact,
From what once seemed good to what now proves best.

—ROBERT BROWNING

THE LIFE AND ACHIEVEMENTS of Carl Laemmle constitute more than an American career of financial success. Carl Laemmle was a pioneer in a business destined to become, even in his day, one of the major industries of our land. He was a motion picture distributer and producer. He was one of the first to sense the value of talking pictures, to further their improvement, and to promote their adoption by exhibitors. He directed no movie drama himself; although he was identified with the picture industry for a quarter of a century, his gifts were not those of a creative artist. He was a business executive of vision, daring and honesty. He was president of the Universal Pictures Corporation, an organization for the existence, growth and prosperity of which he himself was mainly responsible.

BACKGROUND AND VOCATIONAL EXPERIENCES

From obscure beginnings Carl Laemmle progressed from one occupation to another until he made for himself a definite and lucrative place in the motion picture industry. He was born in 1867 in Laupheim, a town of some three thousand inhabitants in the South German kingdom of Wüttenberg. Carl was the tenth of thirteen children. His father, Julius Baruch Laemmle, was a country real estate agent, a thrifty speculator in small tracts of land. He was highly respected by his fellow townsmen. He acted as arbiter in many family disputes. Once a year the Laemmle family traveled to Ulm, sixteen miles distant, to hear an opera and perchance to see the great Wagner himself.

As a boy Carl displayed no intellectual precocity. He was sent to school when he was six and attended for seven years. For the next three or four years he worked for S. G. Heller, a dealer in stationery goods and novelties, wholesale and retail, in Ichenhausen, a small town forty miles from Laupheim. Mr. Heller, who was a pensioned school teacher, taught Carl arithmetic, grammar and a little English. Carl became bookkeeper and office manager of the Heller business organization. The principles of business which he learned were sound and practical.

Meanwhile, Carl's mind was fired with speculations and enthusiasms for that El Dorado known as America. His brother Joseph had gone to America, and he wrote letters glowing with accounts of opportunities in New York and Chicago for industrious and ambitious young men. Visitors from America opened vistas of social and commercial advantages. Julius Baruch Laemmle gave his son Carl a steerage ticket to New York for his seventeenth birthday. Carl sailed from Bremerhaven with high hopes.

In the course of time Carl Laemmle developed into another Horatio Alger character. He rose from the lowly status of a poor immigrant boy to that of a rich and powerful industrialist. America was indeed the land of opportunity, the land where the paths to fortune were numerous and wide open. The atmosphere was saturated with invitations to young men of enterprise and courage.

Carl Laemmle the immigrant lad worked for the keeper of a drug store on East Thirty-sixth Street in New York at four dollars a week. Carl ran errands, washed bottles, swept the floor. He did not like his work. One day he received a letter from his brother in Chicago with a railroad ticket from New York and ten dollars. Carl went to the Middle West to seek his fortune.

His experiences in the open spaces were varied, if not always exciting. He was employed by a farmer whose land was twenty miles from Yankton, South Dakota.

Carl went to Chicago. Here he worked as a junior entry clerk for Mr. Butler, a hardware merchant. He and his brother Joseph returned to their native town, Laupheim, Germany, in 1886. After an absence of five months Carl returned to Chicago with only one nickel in his pocket. He was employed by Mr. Butler as senior entry clerk at nine dollars a week.

After sundry experiences which we need not recount, Carl went to Oshkosh, Wisconsin, as a bookkeeper in the local branch of the Continental Clothing Company. In a few years he was made manager. He issued a new catalogue which was widely distributed in Wisconsin counties. Mail-order business grew with dramatic rapidity. When a rival clothing merchant offered a turkey at the Thanksgiving season to every purchaser of eight dollar's worth of goods, Laemmle recklessly met and overwhelmed competition by giving a turkey to the buyer of two and a half dollar's worth of merchandise. No profits were registered for Continental by this strategy, but competitors learned not to arouse the antagonism of Laemmle. As manager, Laemmle learned the principles of showmanship which in later years he applied in advertising motion pictures.

Running true to the romantic tradition of the times, Laemmle met Recha, a niece of Sam Stern, the head of the business. She had recently come from Germany. They fell in love and were married in 1898. The happy union was broken by her death twenty-one years later. Not quite in keeping with the guiding expectations of the day was Laemmle's discharge by Stern for requesting a larger share of the profits of the Oshkosh branch's business. The loss of his position occasioned anguish in the breast of Laemmle, but it was a blessing in disguise. It was the turning point in his career. He and his wife returned to Chicago where he engaged in the business that gave full scope to his abilities and raised him to a position of power and prestige in American industry.

He Makes a Place for Himself as a Producer

Carl Laemmle was in Chicago on his thirty-ninth birthday, which occurred on January 17, 1906. He had been weighing and comparing the commercial possibilities of chain five-and-ten-cent stores and of motion pictures. He decided that motion pictures offered him the greater scope for his abilities. Vacant property on Milwaukee Avenue was rented within a month and converted into a five-cent picture house, or a nickelodeon. The building was painted white and called "The White Front." He kept it clean inside. He made a highly successful bid for feminine patronage. Shortly after he opened "The Family Theater." Carl Laemmle was not content to be a successful exhibitor of moving pictures. He had visions of other opportunities associated with the film industry, then still in its infancy.

In the same year he launched The Laemmle Film Service. He distributed films to theater proprietors. In three years this business was the largest of its kind in the world. The next step in Laemmle's career was logical and almost inevitable.

The producers had formed a powerful trust. It was evident that if the corporation found it more profitable to distribute its films through other outlets and agencies, the Laemmle Film Service would collapse. In 1909 Carl Laemmle incorporated a producing firm under the name of "The Yankee Films Company." Passing through progressive stages it finally emerged in 1912 as the strong and influential Universal Pictures Corporation. Laemmle was motivated by the conviction that in order to maintain himself in the film business he must produce pictures himself and induce exhibitors to show them in defiance of the Trust. He formulated a plan that was daring and realized it with a brilliance that wrote a thrilling chapter in American industry.

He engaged in the gigantic undertaking of dissolving by legal process the Trust that threatened his business and personal prestige. In less than three years Laemmle figured in two hundred and eighty-nine actions. The film world was amazed when he was victorious in all suits. To be sure, ways and means were contrived by his opponents to confute, dismay, embarrass and thwart Laemmle. Rumors designed to discredit him were circulated. Violence was resorted to in a desperate attempt to accomplish his commercial ruin. In 1915 the United States government ordered the Film Trust to abandon all illegal practices. The court decision resulted in the reduction of the Trust to its constituent units. Laemmle had won his place in the warm sun of the open and free film market.

Another remarkable effort was his pioneer attempt to introduce talking pictures to the American people. In the summer of 1928 he installed talking equipment in a theater in Evansville, Indiana, which attracted crowded houses all the summer despite warm weather. Laemmle was the holder of the American agency of the German manufacturers of the synchroscope. That talking pictures rapidly retired the silent films is known to all who are conversant with the modern history of the industry.

Laemmle proceeded from one daring venture to another. He realized a dream which he had cherished for years when, under his direction, the first community ever to be devoted exclusively to the production of motion pictures was organized. Universal City was formally opened in 1915 with appropriate ceremonies.

Laemmle never forgot the poor, the outcast, the distressed. He instigated the practice of exhibiting pictures for the inmates of Sing Sing prison. He offered a prize of fifty dollars for the best title suggested by a convict for a picture shown as "The Photoplay Without a Name." From the four thousand titles submitted, "Polly's Crucible" was deemed the most fitting. The prize winner gave ten of the fifty dollars to the welfare association of the prison.

Laemmle did much for the improvement of the lot of the underprivileged other than through the medium of pictures he produced. He did good even by stealth. He gave more than one derelict a second chance. Samuel M. Osborn, then warden of Sing Sing, sought suitable positions for men who were discharged from prison with satisfactory records. Laemmle volunteered to provide jobs for two such ex-convicts. They were given opportunities to prove their worth under new names. Their past was as if it had never existed. Both men amply justified the confidence which Laemmle reposed in them.

It is small wonder that Carl Laemmle was regarded as the dean of the producers. As intimated above, he was not a director, not a scenario writer, not an actor. He was an organizer, executive and administrator, possessed of vision and contagious enthusiasm, with a courage that bordered on audacity. Men of his business ability are indispensable in our complex society.

AN EVALUATION OF MOTION PICTURES

What is a fair appraisal of the talking motion pictures to the production and promotion of which he gave himself? One thinks immediately of the improvement of and the stimulus to photography which the film world has occasioned. Technical advances in this area have been transferred to other spheres. To what extent photography would have been further developed and employed in such fields as astronomy and medicine if motion pictures had not been invented, no one can say. That photography as a whole has been expanded and refined under the influence of the motion picture industry none should be disposed to deny.

In the next place, the motion picture has provided gainful employment for an army of people with a wide range of abilities. The film careers of not a few have been lucrative. In a machine age the invention, production and wide distribution of new products are among the prerequisites of the economic prosperity of the nation as a whole. That uncounted individuals with neither the requisite background nor the technical skills have been thwarted and embittered in their attempts to identify themselves with the picture industry can not be successfully disputed. More people have doubtless aspired to cinema careers than the industry could absorb, but nevertheless, multitudes have secured suitable positions in all sorts of aspects of the picture business.

Motion pictures have indirectly created a barrage of magazines which offer their buyers the pageantry of the current critical times in graphic and pictorial forms. The vendors of these periodicals offer a bewildering assortment from which the customer may make his selections. No doubt some journals have been stimulated to improve the illustrations they carry. On the other hand, many leading monthlies continue to issue their contributions without illustrations.

What can be said for the product itself? It must be admitted that, in many instances, crude and elementary standards of taste have prevailed. Perhaps it was to be expected that a new form of amusement that depended for its existence and prosperity on its appeal to the masses should not move on the highest ethical and artistic levels. Much has been done to correct this defect. Under Mr. Will Hays a code regulating the quality of motion pictures was adopted by producing companies. The agreement provides that law, human and natural, is not to be ridiculed; that decent moral standards, subject only to the requirements of drama, are to be presented; and that the sympathy of an audience is not to be aroused for crime or evil. The moral tone of the pictures has been and is being improved.

Outspoken and intelligent critics deplore the false conception of life which many pictures present, even more than they would condemn indecencies and immoralities inflicted upon impressionable persons. For example, the role of romantic love may be too far-extended and overweighted. Love between a young man and woman is deemed sufficient for all exigencies of living. Again, wealth and social position are too frequently conferred by an event little short of fortuitous chance. In other words, the criticism is leveled at the motion pictures that they lack discrimination, a sense of proportion and balance, and thus impart a philosophy of life which leaves its adherents in the lurch when they are face to face with realities.

The possibilities of talking motion pictures have by no means been fully realized. To be sure, many of the plays which only a minor fraction of our people could see on the legitimate stage have been filmed and released as sound pictures in almost every hamlet in the land. Many literary masterpieces have been converted into film dramas. Furthermore, historic figures and occasions have been re-created by the motion picture industry and the presentations have played an influential part in shaping public opinion. Scientific achievements which benefit humanity have been introduced in pictorial form to multitudes who would never consult the literature recording such accomplishments. There is yet much land to be possessed.

Laemmle was among the first to regret the defects and blemishes of the motion pictures and among the first to support constructive criticism and measures for improvement. He solicited fruitful comment and suggestion. He rejoiced in the progress that the motion picture industry made and was justly proud of the part he played in its development and expansion.

In 1939 Laemmle died at the age of seventy-two. The affectionate esteem in which he was held by thousands who knew him intimately and personally was expressed in the democratic salutation, "Uncle Carl."

For Discussion

1. Recall three motion pictures which have appealed to you. What are the characteristics of these which account for the impression made on you?

2. It is said that many people go to the picture shows in an effort to escape boredom and harsh realities. To what extent do you condemn and approve the practice?

3. Do you like double features? Give reasons for your answer.

4. In what ways can motion pictures contribute to the diffusion of useful knowledge?

For Further Reading

Laemmle, Carl, "From the Inside," *Saturday Evening Post*, August and September, 1927, Vol. 200, No. 9, pp. 10 ff., No. 10, pp. 18 ff., No. 11, pp. 28 ff.
Drinkwater, John, *The Life and Adventures of Carl Laemmle*, G. P. Putnam's Sons, New York, 1931.

Felix Adler

Founder of the Society for Ethical Culture

by

KENDIG BRUBAKER CULLY

The creed thy father built, wherein his soul
Did live and move and find its vital joy,
May be but small to thee; then, without fear,
Build o'er again the atrium of the soul
So broad that all mankind may feast with thee.

—WILLIAM O. PARTRIDGE

LIKE SO MANY OTHERS among America's leading thinkers, Felix Adler was the product of European roots. His father, a Jewish rabbi who later became head of Temple Emanu-El, New York City, came to this country in 1857 from Germany, where his son had been born at Alzey on August 13, 1851.

Home influences must have gone far to create intellectual curiosity in the youth. It goes without saying that his pious family held forth the rabbinate to him as a supreme life-goal. They were interested in books and culture, and the young man soon developed similar interests. Another influence affected him profoundly. Often he would accompany his mother into the slums of New York on errands of mercy.

The outward events in Adler's life were not spectacular in any great degree. He became known chiefly as the founder of a modern ethical movement. Thus we shall find his particular genius to lie in the realm of thought rather than in action. Of action, however, there was enough. Felix Adler would have objected to being considered a cloistered thinker. The Altogether Good was the Holy Grail which he sought all his years.

STUDENT

Adler enrolled as a student in the Columbia Grammar School of New York. Later he took his Bachelor of Arts degree in Columbia College, in 1870. Then he went to Europe for further study. He tarried at Berlin, and Heidelberg University conferred the doctorate in philosophy upon him in March, 1873. Throughout these years of formal academic life, he developed and maintained studious habits, with a particular flair for philosophy. He came to be a firm believer in the discipline of education. The story is told that when he became a full-fledged doctor, he let his friends know in no uncertain terms that henceforth he preferred to be called Doctor Adler. This was not the sort of pedantic arrogance it would seem to imply. Socially and intellectually, Adler was a humble man. He was simply pleased that now he should have acquired the right to speak with authority on matters congenial to himself.

Early in life he came to believe in a principle which remained fundamental in all his thinking: that every human being is an end in himself and worth while on his own account. He had his first large-scale opportunity to test this principle during his studies abroad. While sojourning in such cities as Paris, Berlin and Vienna, he observed how many students held a coarse and degrading attitude toward women, whom they frequently regarded as existing chiefly for their personal gratification. Adler refused to let himself be goaded into similar attitudes, even though his fellows seldom understood his desire for "purity."

Another tendency which arose in his thinking at this time was an increasing skepticism concerning traditional ideas of religion which he had acquired at home and in school. He could no longer accept the creation doctrine as set forth in Genesis, nor did he like the idea of representing God in terms of human attributes. His studies of the great philosopher of Germany, Immanuel Kant, led him to think in terms of ethics rather than of theology. He became convinced the moral law should replace the God-idea.

He happened to read a book by Friedrich Albert Lange, entitled *The Labor Question.* This book was a turning point in his career. Lange introduced the student to the great economic and social

problems which working men were facing. Adler was fired with
a new enthusiasm, he would return to America as the prophet of
the Moral Law. He would call the privileged classes to repentance
because of their treatment of the laborers. He would do something
constructive to lift the workers' level of living.

Meanwhile the young student was undergoing a spiritual transformation. We have referred already to his increasing skepticism
with regard to theism. That was the beginning of a growing dis-
satisfaction with the Hebrew tradition in which he had been
nurtured. His break with the faith of his fathers was not sudden.
He felt that it was a smooth and gradual transition to what he
deemed a higher faith. He did not lose respect for those whom
he called the Old Masters in religion. He felt a particularly strong
kinship, in fact, to the Hebrew prophets because they had made
the first strong ethical advances. Yet he came to believe that the
Hebrew principles were not adaptable to the modern need for uni-
versals in religion; he found the doctrine of the chosen people
repugnant to his desire for this universality. He also felt that the
tradition of Israel stressed too much the negative aspects of justice,
such as doing away with oppression, which in itself he thought
could not affect the desired synthesis.

By the time Adler was ready to return home, he must have
reached a momentous decision—not to become a rabbi. His final
action was bound up with a matter of biblical interpretation. At
one point in the Sabbath service, the rabbi holds up the Pentateuch
scroll and recites: "And this is the Law which Moses set before
the people of Israel." His studies in modern biblical criticism had
introduced him to the scholarly hypothesis that Moses could not
have been solely responsible for this Law, which is instead a com-
posite of many strains in Hebrew life. He decided that he could
not sincerely officiate in these words at a service in the synagogue.

BACK HOME

His first act upon returning from abroad was to join several
friends in organizing a society which they called the "Union for
the Higher Life." Three principles united them: sex purity; de-
voting the surplus of one's income beyond that required for one's

own genuine needs to the elevation of the working classes; continued intellectual development. In the same spurt of enthusiasm he was instrumental in establishing a co-operative printing shop, which failed; and the Workingman's School, designed to foster a co-operative spirit among laborers.

The intellectual pace continued unabated. He had accepted the professorship of Hebrew and Oriental Literature in Cornell University, where he remained for three years. His scholarly life gave him adequate opportunity to continue his spiritual quest. For a while he was influenced by Emersonian principles. He had met Ralph Waldo Emerson in 1875, thereafter mingling intimately with others who had been influenced by the Sage of Concord. He read the *Essays* again and again. The stress in Emerson which Adler found congenial was his lofty conception of the self, with its power for experiencing the divine power within itself. Yet he finally differed with Emerson in coming to believe that the individual self is more important than merely serving as a vehicle for the One. He also felt that Emerson's ideas overlooked the importance of service to humanity by way of correcting social ills.

Next he turned to the New Testament. He wanted to know more about Jesus' ethical teachings. Contrary to those who said that Jesus was not original, Adler found in Jesus' teachings two altogether unique principles: nonviolent resistance and love as the meaning of the forgiveness of enemies. In spite of his strong attraction to some of Jesus' teachings, Adler could not bring himself to the point of confessing Christianity. He did not like either the Christian emphasis on the person of Christ or Jesus' evident belief in the coming end of the world. Jesus had gone far, he thought, but the final word about ethics had not been spoken by the Nazarene.

At this point he began to stress the necessity of overcoming social evils. He conceived a new purpose in living as lying in the process of eradicating such evils as prostitution and the exploitation of laborers. For a time he indulged in Utopian dreams, contemplating the perfect society on earth. He introduced Henry George of Single Tax fame the first time that leader was presented to New York's public, but he never became a Single Tax advocate. He read Karl Marx's *Das Kapital* with interest. He was in sympathy with socialism's desire to relieve the suffering of the poor. However, he thought socialism failed to detect the moral factor in the cause of poverty. It talked in dialectical terms, and Adler was primarily interested in a religious approach to the personal ethical choices of men and women.

Eventually he reached a satisfying conclusion. He himself called it the "three-fold reverence." Dominating the ethical life of a person should be: 1. Reverence for the precious, permanent, ethical achievements of the past and for those who achieved them, the Old Masters. 2. Reverence for those approximately on the same level of life as ourselves, but whose gifts are different from and supplementary to ours. 3. Reverence for the undeveloped, including backward groups among civilized peoples as well as uncivilized peoples.

Now Felix Adler was ready for his great life work: the institutional expression of his convictions.

The Society for Ethical Culture

The social manifestation of Adler's ethical principles is the Society for Ethical Culture, of which he was the acknowledged founder. The Society had its start on May 15, 1876, when a hundred or so people gathered in a hall in New York. They had come to hear Professor Adler of Cornell University outline his proposal for a religious society free from creed, devoted only to the pursuit of ethical truth. Adler later expressed the feeling of this group. They were asking what consecrating influence could be brought into their lives, and into the lives of their children. They were mostly people who had found the older religious expression unsatisfactory to themselves. They had now no desire to combat the older forms of Christianity and Judaism, but they wanted to venture into new and fresh pastures of the spirit.

Sunday meetings were instituted at Standard Hall. There was no ritual. Music was introduced in order to create an atmosphere of reverent thought. Attention, however, was focused primarily on an address by some teacher. The Ethical Culture teacher would have to be skilled in the humanistic sciences, understanding with regard to the whole history of man's spiritual quests, and convinced regarding the new synthesis the Society was striving to achieve.

Joseph Seligman, a wealthy and respected New Yorker, was the first President of the Society. Through his instrumentalities, the interest of many was aroused in the youthful Society. It has frequently been pointed out that Jews predominated in the membership of the group, although its teachers were more frequently non-Jewish. The Society aimed to be open to all, regardless of racial or religious background.

Although the group was later to receive encouragement from liberal leaders in church and synagogue, even though these were not in agreement with its nontheistic positions, at first it was attacked violently. Fundamentalist Christians denounced it in scathing terms. Outright materialists made their attack from another angle—they called it "vaguely idealistic." The movement has never spread widely in terms of its number of adherents. Its appeal has remained intellectualistic, although Adler was always careful to warn against overintellectualization of any kind.

People in other cities became interested. Local groups were formed in various communities, notably Philadelphia, Chicago, St. Louis, and Boston. These local societies federated in 1889 as the American Ethical Union, a sort of clearinghouse of inspiration, information, and promotion, as well as a publishing agency. The Union instituted a journal, *The Ethical Record,* which later became the *International Journal of Ethics,* still a prominent publication but now published under other auspices. Summer schools of ethics were established in Plymouth, Massachusetts; Madison, Wisconsin; and elsewhere.

In 1896 an International Union of Ethical Societies was founded, since by then the movement had spread abroad. It must have been immensely satisfying to Adler to see his interests extending into the countries where he had spent precious years of study. A Congress of Ethical Societies was held at Zurich in 1896, and a subsequent congress at Eisenach in 1906. As a result of the latter meeting, an International Congress on Moral Education was held at London in 1908, sponsored and attended by governmental min-

isters of education and representatives of leading universities from
many parts of the world. This international emphasis of the
Ethical Culture Societies has continued across the years, since it is
based on the conviction that ethical truth is supraracial and supra-
nationalistic.

The insight and genius of Felix Adler lay back of this whole
developing movement. Brilliant teachers emerged, such as Walter
L. Sheldon, William M. Salter, S. Burns Weston, Percival Chubb,
David S. Muzzey, and Stanton Coit. Adler remained the First
Teacher.

APPLIED ETHICS

Always interested in applied ethics, Adler was continually doing
creative things. In the same year the Society for Ethical Culture
was established, he started the first public kindergarten west of
the Mississippi, in San Francisco. In order to impart the Society's
ideals to youth, he opened the Ethical Culture School in New
York, which has attracted wide attention as a center of progressive
educational techniques. In 1884 he served as a member of the
State Tenement House Commission. Working with Edmond Kelly,
he organized the Good Government Club, which later developed
into the City Club of New York. He helped agitate for improved
conditions among the East Side's poor. He served as chairman of
the National Child Labor Committee, and helped end a strike
among 60,000 workers in the garment-making industry.

His scholarly interests continued as well. In 1902 he returned
to Columbia, his Alma Mater, as Professor of Political and Social
Ethics. He was invited to be Theodore Roosevelt Professor in the
University of Berlin and to deliver the world-famous Hibbert Lectures in Oxford University.

Loved by thousands, internationally celebrated, he died in 1933.
Father of five children, brother-in-law of Mr. Justice Louis Dembitz Brandeis, he had had a rich domestic life, concerning which
the public had known little. Chiefly, however, Felix Adler will be
remembered by posterity as the founder of a movement.

For Discussion

1. Evaluate the ethical principles for which Felix Adler stood. Point out which of these stem from (a) Judaism; (b) Christianity; (c) other sources.

2. Try to discover the principles of education followed by the Ethical Culture School.

3. In what respect does Felix Adler's relation to the Society for Ethical Culture differ from Mary Baker Eddy's relation to the Church of Christ, Scientist?

4. Do you think that recent world developments invalidate Felix Adler's principles?

5. How do you think a fundamentalist Christian would react to the Ethical Culture movement? (b) a liberal Christian? (c) an orthodox Jew? (d) a liberal Jew? (e) a humanist? (f) a Buddhist?

6. What dangers are involved in a purely ethical conception of religion? Do you think that a high ethical religion can be maintained if God is removed from the center of life?

For Further Reading

Adler, Felix, *An Ethical Philosophy of Life Presented in Its Main Outlines*, D. Appleton and Company, New York, 1918. (Autobiographical Introduction).

————, *Life and Destiny; or, Thoughts from the Ethical Lectures of Felix Adler*, Watts, London, 1913.

————, *Marriage and Divorce*, McClure, Phillips and Company, New York, 1905.

————, *The Essentials of Spirituality*, J. Pott and Company, New York, 1905.

————, *The Moral Instruction of Children*, D. Appleton and Company, New York, 1892.

————, *The Reconstruction of the Spiritual Ideal*, (Hibbert Lectures, 1923), D. Appleton and Company, New York, 1924.

————, *The World Crisis and Its Meaning*, D. Appleton and Company, New York, 1915.

Bridges, Horace James, (ed.) *Aspects of Ethical Religion;* Essays in Honor of Felix Adler on the Fiftieth Anniversary of His Founding of the Ethical Movement, 1876. American Ethical Union, New York, 1926.

Louis Dembitz Brandeis

Justice of the Supreme Court

by

KENDIG BRUBAKER CULLY

He hath showed thee, O man, what is good;
and what doth the Lord require of thee,
but to do justly, and to love kindness,
and to walk humbly with thy God?

—MICAH 6:8

LOUIS DEMBITZ BRANDEIS will be remembered in the annals of American history in more than one way. Doubtless, his tenure as Associate Justice of the Supreme Court of the United States will be the focal point of his fame. That, however, was in many respects merely the culmination of his career. As we shall observe, his roots of influence extend deeply into several areas of our national life.

THE BEGINNINGS

This man was born on November 13, 1856, in Louisville, Kentucky, a city he was destined to regard with affection all his days, although the locale of his labors was to take him far from his birthplace. His father and mother, Adolf and Frederika (Dembitz) Brandeis, had come to Louisville only a few years earlier from Prague, Bohemia. They were but two among thousands of immigrants who came to these shores because of the economic and political confusion existent in continental Europe at that time. Appreciative of the free opportunities they found here, they had had little difficulty in adjusting themselves to their new situation. The business which Adolf Brandeis established as a grain merchant in 1851 prospered, and by the time of Louis' birth the family were economically comfortable.

In his home the youth had the stimulus of lofty conversation, good books, music, and a circle of sensitive and intelligent friends. At an early age he learned to play the violin, with his sister Fanny serving as his instructor. He came to venerate an uncle, Lewis Dembitz, who occupied a place of prominence in Louisville as a lawyer. In fact, the boy, who had been christened Louis David, later chose to adopt "Dembitz" as his middle name, in token of the esteem wherein he held his uncle.

In 1872, when Louis was sixteen, threats of a financial depression led his father to relinquish some of his business interests. Taking advantage of the lull in affairs, the family sailed for Europe on a prolonged vacation. To the impressionable youth this journey was intensely meaningful. During the next two years he was enrolled as a student in the Annen-Realschule, Dresden. There he acquired an intimate knowledge of several languages. More important than the cultural values inhering in such a sojourn, however, were the new pulls be began to feel toward his homeland. By contrast with ancient Europe, the Ohio Valley seemed to the young man all the more inviting. So, when his father urged him to stay in Europe and to take up medical studies, Louis the more firmly turned his footsteps homeward. Furthermore, he had no inclinations toward medicine. For many years he had aspired to be a lawyer.

The next step was Harvard Law School, which he entered in 1875. Although he had liked Louisville, Boston and its environs soon proved to be even more appealing. Forever afterwards he was to consider Massachusetts his home. Brandeis was enamored of the type of culture which Harvard and Boston were able to offer him. They were made for him, as he was for them.

At Harvard Brandeis attracted attention because of his brilliant academic capacities, as well as by his penchant for genuine friendship. He was an indefatigable student. At one point during these years his eyes seemed to go back on him. Fearing some serious maladjustment, he consulted a New York specialist, who told him simply not to use his eyes unduly. Back at school, his friends were persuaded to read to him, in order to supplement his visual deficiency.

He showed early evidences in Harvard of a habit of frugality which was to remain with him as a salient characteristic. He reduced his personal needs to the barest minimum in order not to waste time and money. By tutoring other students he was able to make quite a sum of money over and above living expenses and school costs. He had had to borrow two hundred dollars in order to enter the Law School. He graduated with fifteen hundred dollars in investments.

Brandeis could not register as a candidate for the law degree, since he did not enter with the prerequisite, a college degree. Yet, because of his brilliant record, he was awarded the law degree *cum laude* by special action of the Trustees. Later, he was invited to teach in Harvard on a part-time basis. In 1891 his Alma Mater recognized distinguished services by conferring upon him the honorary degree of Master of Arts.

Graduation, of course, meant the beginning of his career. His first venture took him to St. Louis, Missouri, whither he went to assume a position in the office of James Taussig. He had high hopes for his work in that city, particularly since well-trained lawyers were scarce, and it appeared that he had a real contribution to make. However, after Boston, St. Louis seemed to him like a veritable outpost. After a few months, he was happy to return to the city of his student days. There he opened a law office in partnership with a classmate, Samuel Dennis Warren, who had become a fast friend. Through influential contacts among their acquaintances, and a growing reputation, the two fared very well. Before long their services were in such demand that they had to increase their staff and office facilities. Apart from vocational success, or parallel with it, Brandeis was becoming financially independent. Across the years, through legitimate work and careful investment, he was able to amass a fortune of approximately two million dollars.

His marriage was singularly fortunate. On a visit to his parents' home in Louisville, Brandeis met Miss Alice Goldmark, a New

Yorker who happened to be visiting in the city. At this time
Brandeis was thirty-four. Within two weeks they were engaged.
Later they discovered that they were second cousins. After their
marriage, the couple continued the simplicity of living, as far
as external arrangements were concerned, which Brandeis had
adopted for himself. Yet their life was rich. Week-ends were
spent at a country place in Dedham, which always was a welcome
retreat from the busy law office. Much later in Washington, Sunday afternoon teas, over which Mrs. Brandeis graciously presided,
were *events* in the life of a small company of friends who gathered
for dignified, profound conversation and fellowship. Their daughters, Susan and Elizabeth, both achieved distinguished academic
records. Susan took up law, studying in the University of Chicago.

REFORM IN BOSTON

Almost from the first, Brandeis was very much involved in matters of public concern. He was possessed of a passionate interest
in social improvements. He conceived the lawyer's task as helping
to maintain the highest public morality. Throughout his career,
he continued a firm believer in due legal processes; but the law appeared to him primarily, in effect, for the protection and the welfare of human beings whose affairs brought it forth. Although he
was always a thoroughgoing scholar, never content with hasty opinion unsupported by evidence, he never became a mere reflection
of his musty shelves of lawbooks.

One of his first concentrated efforts lay in the direction of improving legal education. Law schools were in a period of transition. Curricula required strengthening. Higher standards for
admission to the bar were imperative. Starting with Harvard, he
initiated tendencies which later were to make American law schools
perhaps the foremost in the world. He foresaw that Harvard Law
School might become the mecca for some of the most promising
students in the country. On the occasion of the two hundred fiftieth
anniversary of Harvard College, the Harvard Law School Association was launched, largely through Brandeis' instrumentality. One

160463

hundred and fifty alumni formed the nucleus of the Association, which soon attracted a membership of eight hundred. Distinguished leaders whom Brandeis interested included Rutherford B. Hayes, Joseph H. Choate, and Chief Justice Fuller. The immediate results were an increased student body, contributions looking toward the establishment of professorships, and the founding of the *Harvard Law Review*.

Soon Brandeis was doing more than serving as corporation counsellor, or defending individual clients, or improving legal education. He was in the thick and thin of Boston's municipal social problems. Through the influence of two women, Elizabeth Glendower Evans and Alice N. Lincoln, philanthropically inclined Bostonians, Brandeis' attention was turned toward the distressing conditions in the city's institutions for the care of the poor. All kinds of derelicts, victims of mental disease, and the economically bereft were treated as a unit, and thrown together under facilities which were poorly supervised and utterly inadequate. No system of rehabilitation existed. For almost a year Brandeis served as Mrs. Lincoln's counsel in hearings before the Board of Aldermen, which finally yielded to logic and aroused public opinion by completely reorganizing the municipal department of public institutions.

At this early juncture in his career, Brandeis established a principle which he followed rigorously: never to accept a fee for public services of this kind. He felt that this was merely his contribution as a private citizen, and not an opportunity for private gain. Income from his regular practice and his investments had freed him from financial concern. This was all to be public service gladly given.

Several situations brought Brandeis into the public eye in such a way as to make him more than a local celebrity. There was the case of private ownership of transportation franchises—a problem not peculiar to Boston. A new subway was proposed for the city. Brandeis was soon in the midst of the struggle to preserve public control of Boston's streets—what was above and what was below them as well. Another situation arose when a private company sought incorporation with a view to constructing freight tunnels in Boston, Cambridge, and Somerville. Still another *cause celebre* was the effort of eight gas companies in the city to consolidate, and in the process to "water" their stock capitalization. Brandeis contended that this action would tend to cause more than their just deserts to accrue to the holders of surplus over the original capital. The argument was produced that such legislation would inhibit free enterprise. Brandeis replied that the capitalists should welcome anti stock-watering legislation "as tending to protect them from the temptation to do injustice." In these struggles the lawyer was assisted by prominent citizens, including Edward A. Filene, wealthy and public-spirited member of a Boston merchandising family.

Brandeis believed firmly in educating the public in order to achieve social reforms, which, he believed, if instigated by a few people, would have little lasting effect. To that end he and others formed the Public Franchise League, which backed the foregoing efforts and, by stimulating public interest in reform, met other exigencies which arose. Politicians and big businessmen had a tendency to be less belligerent when their constituencies developed opinions of their own.

RADICAL?

At various points in his career, Brandeis was branded socialistic or communistic. He was rapidly developing the reputation of being a radical. His opponents spread malicious fabrications concerning his motives and methods. He was accused frequently of having accepted bribes, or huge retaining fees, in the guise of public interest. In one period, the negative honor came to him of having a weekly magazine in Boston established, avowedly in order to lambaste him. In one issue of the magazine, which was called *Truth,* a cartoon represents him with hands in attitude of prayer and with a halo about his head, and the label is "St. Louis of Boston."

These attacks rarely disturbed him unduly. He knew that they were the inevitable accompaniment of any high-minded devotion to the commonweal. He never replied in kind. In fact, it was debated from time to time across the years as to whether Louis Brandeis was liberal or conservative. There was never any ready-made reply forthcoming. Brandeis always sought to be, and was, above labels. Politically, this was true also. In party affiliation he was Democratic most of the time. Sometimes, however, he supported Republicans or Independents. His choice was always the candidate best suited, in his mind, to the tasks at hand.

The contribution which Brandeis considered his greatest labor of love was Massachusetts' Savings Bank Life Insurance. Life insurance companies were coming to be scrutinized closely. It was alleged that their financial policies were open to suspicion. From the investment standpoint, they were linked very often with big business, and investigations of their practices disclosed that in many cases individuals were paying exorbitant fees for the protection the companies offered. For months Brandeis pursued a campaign to educate the public concerning these abuses. He offered as a substitute a system of life insurance to be made available through the state-controlled savings banks. Even the savings banks themselves were loath to take it up. In 1907 legislative action established the plan, and the following year it began to function. Progress was slow, but caution led to its financial success. Brandeis' faith was vindicated. During the depression of the 'twenties, the system stood up without the loss of a cent to its policyholders.

Brandeis became a national figure when he entered the anti trust field. One by one also he took up cudgels for other worth-while causes. He defended labor's right to a share in the profits caused by the introduction of labor-saving machinery. He worked hard to make labor and capital recognize each other as mutually related in a common destiny. He studied consumers' co-operatives, and urged their extension. He opposed the high tariffs which inhibited free trade. After initial questionings, he became an advocate of woman suffrage.

Eventually, in spite of a definite antipathy toward becoming involved in campaign politics, he did feel it his duty to take the "stump" for Woodrow Wilson. President Wilson was later to appoint him to the highest tribunal of the land.

SUPREME COURT JUSTICE

The Supreme Court appointment came to him unexpectedly, but he accepted it without hesitation. The only regret he and Mrs. Brandeis felt was the necessity of their leaving Dedham to go to Washington permanently. His confirmation by the Senate as Associate Justice was a vindication of his pre-eminent qualification for this high office. He had been decidedly anathema to large sections of the reactionary and conservative groups. When his nomination was announced, immediately a stream of protest came to the Senate Judiciary Committee from his enemies. He was branded as lacking the "judicial temperament." Distinguished fellow barristers registered their opinion that he ought not to be seated. The final vote was 47 yea; 22 nay. Many years later, after Louis Brandeis had distinguished himself on all scores in the Court, one of the Senators who had voted against his appointment, the late William E. Borah of Idaho, voiced the sentiment of many others of his colleagues when he publicly stated that he regretted that negative vote in 1916.

During his years on the Supreme Court—he was sixty when appointed—Brandeis continued loyal to his unwavering principles. Perforce he was now no longer free to be the reformer or advocate. However, he enjoyed the opportunity to have a part in the actual making of judicial history. To him the law was rooted in human needs; the jurist's function was to interpret the Constitution in terms of changing social situations. During much of his tenure, he was a liberal in a conservative court. However, the years produced changes in personnel which brought other liberals to his side. And the friendship of Mr. Justice Oliver Wendell Holmes, with whom he did not always agree, judicially speaking, buoyed him up in remarkable degree, whenever difficulties mounted.

HUMANITARIAN

No account of the life of Louis Dembitz Brandeis would be complete without reference to his interest in Zionism—the movement to restore Palestine as the Jewish homeland. His participation in this movement came at an advanced stage of his career, in a sort of conversion experience which suddenly made him cognizant of the great Jewish heritage in which he shared. He had never been, nor never came to be, pious in the sense of attending synagogue services; his religion was humanistic rather than theocentric. Yet he came to have a growing sensitiveness to the Hebrew ethical stream to which he felt a spiritual kinship. He was placed high in Zionist counsels. At one time he visited Palestine, the land whose future seemed to him and others such an amazing opportunity. After his own awakening, he was surprised and delighted to find that his own uncle, the beloved Lewis Dembitz, was held in high esteem by those to whom things Jewish were revered.

Finally, he turned his attention once more to his not-forgotten home city of Louisville. In company with his brother Alfred he undertook a project to enhance the University of Louisville. He believed that sectional culture was an essential part of American life. To the end of widening the interest of Kentuckians in their own illustrious past and promising future, he sought to build up the University libraries. As a result of counsel and financial aid, the Brandeis family have helped to create a truly notable series of libraries in Louisville.

In 1939 Louis Dembitz Brandeis retired from the Supreme Court of the United States, aged eighty-three. He died on October 5, 1941.

For Discussion

1. To what extent do you think Brandeis' early life influenced his later development?

2. Were there justifiable bases for opposing Brandeis' appointment to the Supreme Court?

3. What penalties by way of curtailed freedom of action does a Supreme Court Justice have to pay by virtue of his office?

4. Brandeis was not active in the worship of the synagogue. Was he religious?

5. What part do you think laws should play in our lives? Was Brandeis right in thinking of law as a "living" thing?

For Further Reading

Brandeis, Louis Dembitz, *Other People's Money and How the Bankers Use It,*
    Frederick A. Stokes and Co., New York, 1914.
Alfred Lief, *The Social and Economic Views of Mr. Justice Brandeis,* Vanguard
    Press, New York, 1930.
Frankfurter, Felix, ed., *Mr. Justice Brandeis,* Essays by Charles E. Hughes, Max
    Lerner, Felix Frankfurter, et al., Yale University Press, New Haven, 1932.
————, *Brandeis: The Personal History of an American Ideal,* Stackpole
    Sons, New York, 1936.
Mason, Alpheus Thomas, *Brandeis: Lawyer and Judge in the Modern State,*
    Princeton University Press, Princeton, 1933.